Bringing technology into the classroom

Bringing technology into the classroom

Gordon Lewis

OXFORD
UNIVERSITY PRESS

OXFORD
UNIVERSITY PRESS

Great Clarendon Street, Oxford OX2 6DP

Oxford University Press is a department of the University of Oxford.
It furthers the University's objective of excellence in research, scholarship,
and education by publishing worldwide in

Oxford New York

Auckland Cape Town Dar es Salaam Hong Kong Karachi
Kuala Lumpur Madrid Melbourne Mexico City Nairobi
New Delhi Shanghai Taipei Toronto

With offices in

Argentina Austria Brazil Chile Czech Republic France Greece
Guatemala Hungary Italy Japan Poland Portugal Singapore
South Korea Switzerland Thailand Turkey Ukraine Vietnam

OXFORD and OXFORD ENGLISH are registered trade marks of
Oxford University Press in the UK and in certain other countries

ISBN: 978 0 19 442594 0

Printed in China

ACKNOWLEDGEMENTS

The publishers would like to thank the following for permission to reproduce photographs:
Microsoft Corporation p.28 (Track Changes on Windows); p.35 Solutions iTools
Elementary, (Main menu and submenu) Oxford University Press; p.37
Solutions iTools Elementary, (Drag and Drop) Oxford University Press; p.38
Project iTools (Hide and Reveal) Oxford University Press; p.50 www.de.licio.us.
com; p.51 RSS feeds logo; p.51 Google Inc (Google Reader); p.57 and p.58 www.
SurveyMonkey.com; p.59 www.easytestmaker.com; p.64 www.edublogs.org;
p.66 wikispaces.com (authors p.70 Apple iTunes; p.77 www.Flickr.com; p.80
and p.81 Ning.com

*Although every effort has been made to trace and contact copyright holders before
publication, this has not been possible in some cases. We apologize for any apparent
infringement of copyright and, if notified, the publisher will be pleased to rectify any
errors or omissions at the earliest opportunity.*

Contents

Contents

Introduction

Educational technology is not new. Almost as long as there have been teachers, there have been instructional tools to help students learn. Clay slates, the abacus, pencils and pens, typewriters, overhead projectors, computers, and finally, the internet, mobile phones, and social networks – there has been an ever accelerating cycle of innovation in teaching tools, yet the classroom challenges have remained essentially the same: how do we 'reach' our students? How can we challenge them and motivate them to think for themselves? How can we use the tools at our disposal to improve the classroom experience?

There is little doubt that new technologies open up possibilities unheard of in previous eras. But these technologies will have only limited impact if the pedagogy behind their application does not keep pace. Technology is nothing without a teacher and a plan.

It is probably safe to say that most educated people will have little difficulty understanding technology basics. In fact, nowadays most of us take the ability to use a word processor, write emails, and search the internet for granted. Even if you don't know how to do such fundamental things as cut and paste text or download a video, there are an infinite number of tutorials available on the internet that will show you how.

The real knowledge gap lies in the application of this new technology. There is still a huge divide between the teaching strategies of the analogue classroom and the digital world in which we live.

This book aims to fill the gap between the potential of technology and current classroom practice. Additional material can be found on the website accompanying the book, (www.oup.com/elt/catalogue/teachersites/itc/btic). Together, the book and the website provide a solid framework for technology integration and practical examples of activities you can use in your classroom to help you, the teacher, to feel confident in making educated choices on introducing and implementing technology.

A word of advice

Don't let yourself feel intimidated by new technology. Don't let new words like wiki, blog, or podcast confuse you. The rapid pace of new developments means that almost everyone is adjusting and learning as they go along. There is no right or wrong way of integrating technology. You don't need to follow the latest trend just because it is there. Standard technologies can in many cases achieve the same or similar results as using more sophisticated applications. Don't worry about being completely up-to-date. New technology is introduced every day. Use what works for you.

The important point to understand is that using technology is not a choice anymore. It is a necessity. In a world full of sights and sounds it would be inappropriate to try and teach through the printed word alone.

Many of your students will be interested in using technology because it is new and exciting. But although it is good to encourage this interest, you also need to bear in mind your language teaching goals.

As you consider implementing technology, always have your ultimate language learning goals clearly in focus. It is very easy for students to get carried away and spend valuable language learning time creating colourful graphics or embedding animations in slide shows which contribute next to nothing to the language learning process. This is not to say that we should discourage students from using technology creatively. It can be a great motivator and help increase students' pride in their work. However, there needs to be a defined language component in each activity if you want to make the task meaningful for your classroom.

Part 1   Developing a technology plan

1 Define your teaching model

This book explores computer **applications** available both on the internet and offline, starting with offline applications such as word processing and presentation software, then exploring the uses of interactive whiteboards (IWBs), before finally looking at uses of the internet in the language teaching classroom. The aim of this book is to demonstrate that technology can enhance your present teaching, without being seen as threateningly 'modern' or replacing what you already know and do.

Before you begin to design a technology plan, you need to consider the overall educational philosophy of your educational establishment. Think about what you consider to be effective teaching. What is your model? Are you task-based? Do you believe in integrated or discrete skills practice? Is authentic content important to you? Does your classroom situation facilitate groupwork? Are your students encouraged to work autonomously?

There is no single objective definition of good teaching practice. It depends to a large extent on your social and educational context as well as the set of core beliefs that motivate your practice. The way you use technology should reflect these beliefs. You will need to look at technology critically and select the tools that best match your needs. This book will help you to do so.

↓ WHAT IS YOUR PERSONAL TECHNOLOGY PROFILE?

Technology experts frequently use the terms 'digital natives' versus 'digital immigrants' when attempting to classify types of technology users. What do these terms mean? Basically, a digital native is someone who has grown up with digital technology (computers, the internet, mobile phones, **MP3** players, etc). A digital immigrant is someone who grew up without digital technology and adopted it as an adult.

Most of our students are probably digital natives, but many of us teachers are to some extent digital immigrants, at least in terms of how we use technology in our language classrooms. But like immigrants who move to another country and culture, it is possible to assimilate into the digital world. One can look at this process of assimilation as taking place in four distinct phases. Read through the descriptions below and decide which phase you would say you fit into.

Newcomer: you never use technology in your daily or professional life. This may be because you have had no access to the technological tools and hence no interest in it. Maybe you are simply a 'technophobe' and feel threatened by technology. Often a lack of access to training can make people feel intimidated by computers.

Casual user: you use technology in your daily life. You can use a word processing programme to write documents and/or lesson plans and you probably use email to correspond with friends and colleagues. You are comfortable searching the internet for information. Although you may have access to computers in your classroom, you only occasionally use them and not according to a plan.

'Old schooler': you have adopted technology into your daily classroom life, but you use it in much the same way you use other more traditional classroom tools. You may create worksheets and handouts for your students or get them to use software programmes to practise and support what they have learnt. Technology coexists with your established lesson plan. It supports and may even extend learning, but does not influence the process.

Innovator: you embrace technology in ways that not only support the learning process but transform it. You use technology to promote learner autonomy and support critical and creative thinking and problem-solving skills. You infuse your lessons with real-life content, promote authentic communication, and provide opportunities to create products with a professional look and feel, and share them with a variety of audiences both local and global.

↓ HOW WELL EQUIPPED IS YOUR SCHOOL?

Your school is the second thing to consider, since it is no use being a technological innovator if there is no or limited computer technology available in your place of work. Even schools with lots of equipment face challenges such as access time and scheduling conflicts. So before you go any further, consider the following questions:

- Is your school connected directly to the internet (by **broadband**) or do you need to dial up to connect (which is slower to operate)? Broadband can handle larger chunks of data so it is better for Web 2.0 applications/activities. (See page 61.)
- Where are your computers located? Are they in your classroom or in a computer room? If the computers are in a computer room, what are the terms of access: do you need to reserve the computers?
- How many computers are available to your students? Can all the students work simultaneously or will you need to split your class up into groups?
- Are all the work stations identically equipped or, for example, do some have internet access and others not?
- Can you share information between computers? Where is student work saved: locally on each work station, or on a central server?
- Are the computers 'locked' or can you add new software (such as photo and video editing, file sharing or video conferencing, or social networking applications) and use peripheral devices such as USB sticks, scanners, video cameras, or MP3 players?

Define your teaching model

- Do you have access to training and technical support? You may need someone who is confident with computer technology for help when you need advice. This can be a colleague. Perhaps your school can nominate someone as technology champion to help out with ICT. You can solve many problems by yourself using online help functions built into the applications you use.

↓ WHAT YOU NEED TO GET STARTED

To operate with technology, the essentials you need are:

A computer
First of all you need a computer with a connection for the internet. You may want to consider a computer with **wireless internet** capabilities. Wireless connections can be very helpful in the classroom as they allow you to use the computers anywhere in the building. To access the internet via a wireless connection you will need to have a router, a small device which you plug into your **modem** or telephone jack.

An internet provider
In order to connect to the internet you need to choose an internet service provider (**ISP**) that offers this service. If you work for a school or other institution, you probably have an ISP already. If not, there is a huge variety of packages to choose from depending on your budget.

An internet connection
When choosing an internet provider you should also think about which type of connection is best for you. Your internet connection is like a 'pipe' through which data flows. With a bigger pipe, more data flows faster to your computer. In order to take advantage of the multimedia possibilities available online, you really should have a broadband connection.

Web browser software
To surf the internet you will need a special programme called a web **browser**. Web browsers contain a number of useful tools such as **bookmarks** (or 'favourites') which allow you to save webpages, and a 'history' function which traces all the **websites** you have accessed. More on web browsers can be found in the chapter on the world wide web (see page 45).

A printer
You will certainly need a printer to print out hard copies of webpages or examples of students' work. It is much easier to read texts on paper than on a screen. If possible, use a colour printer for final projects or display purposes and a black and white printer to use for printing out students' working copies.

Things that are useful and motivating to have are:

A webcam
A **webcam** is a camera attached to your computer which allows you to have video chats. There is a huge range of webcams to choose from, from very simple models which offer low resolution images to quite expensive

Define your teaching model

models with very clear pictures. If you want to conduct whole-class webcam activities, it is worth investing in a quality webcam with high enough resolution to provide a clear picture on a large screen.

A digital camera

Photographs are a popular resource in most language learning classrooms. Digital images are incredibly useful because of their versatility. Use them on-screen or print them out to create flashcards, posters, or any other traditional materials you decide to use. With the help of photo-editing software you can manipulate images to create customized pictures, sometimes with startling effects (for example, you could create an image showing your students standing on top of the Great Wall of China). Using digital images can really bring out the creativity in your classroom.

Digital cameras have become much more affordable since their introduction in the early years of this century. However, you should consider the number of **megapixels** the camera can produce before buying the cheapest bargain. The higher the number of megapixels, the better the photograph resolution will be. This is important if you want to print large copies.

A scanner

If you can't afford a good digital camera, a scanner is the next best thing. A scanner is a digital copy machine. Good scanners can scan documents, drawings, and photographs with high degrees of resolution and turn them into electronic files. Scanners are particularly useful if you want to create a record of student work, such as an e-portfolio. Also, with a scanner you can work offline and record the results electronically.

A digital video camera

While this is not a must, a video camera can add a whole new level of motivation and excitement to your classroom. Digital video cameras are easy to edit with, have no messy tape, and allow digital movies to be played via your computer, **uploaded** to the internet, or burnt onto a DVD. The one drawback of digital video is that it takes up a lot of memory on your computer and can load very slowly if you have not got a broadband internet connection.

Other additional programmes

Winzip/Stuffit (for Mac): these programmes allow you to 'compress' or **zip** large files for sending and expand them again on the destination computer.

↓ ORGANIZING YOUR CLASSROOM

How you organize your classroom will first and foremost be dictated by the number of computers available to your students and the size of the room. It is unlikely that you will have one computer for each student, so you will need to assume either that more than one student will access the computers at any given time, or that you will divide the class up into groups and have students access the computers in cycles.

If you only have one computer in the classroom, it is very important to link it to a projector so that the whole class can share in any activity. Interactive whiteboards, which we discuss later in this book, are particularly useful in the one-computer classroom. While having just one computer does limit interactivity, you can still conduct text, voice, and audio communications, giving individual students alternating control of the mouse, keyboard, or interactive pen.

If you have more than one computer, you may want to consider using one computer for whole-class presentation with an interactive whiteboard, while distributing the rest of the computers throughout the room as work stations.

Be sure to check where your electrical outlets are located. You will need to keep wires hidden and out of the way of your students. Consider labelling the wires, so you can reconnect them easily if you ever have to move the computers. Also, keep your computers away from windows to prevent glare from sunlight reflecting on the screens.

Think about what you want to do on each computer. Will you have students working simultaneously on the same tasks or can you assign students to specific computers for different activities, i.e. word processing, internet search, listening, layout/design? If you have limited access to software, printers, or other peripherals, you will need to bear this in mind in distributing tasks.

↓ LITERACY AND INFORMATION AND COMMUNICATION TECHNOLOGY (ICT)

With the growth of ICT, the concept of literacy has changed dramatically. Literacy now extends well beyond the written word. Today, there is not one literacy, but multiple literacies for students to master when using new technology tools and accessing the internet. Some writers group all these literacies together under the umbrella term 'digital literacy', but the definition is fluid. Below are three core new literacies which must be considered for your classroom.

Computer literacy

In order to function in today's world, an understanding of how computers work is a basic skill, just as holding a pencil is. These skills include manipulating a mouse, formatting and printing a document, searching the web, or playing audio and video on a computer. Today, most students are to a great degree computer literate, but you should not take this for granted. Just as we discussed your own technology profile, be sure to check your students' computer skills before deciding on which technology to introduce.

Information literacy

While most students are computer literate, the level of information literacy is less developed – and this is cause for major concern. The internet has exposed all of us to an almost endless stream of information. Since much of the information on the internet is not reviewed or edited, students need to look critically at what they are accessing (see Figure 1.1 on p.18 below). Unfortunately, many students search randomly and tend to take information from the internet without really reflecting on the source. There is a disturbing trend towards cutting and pasting hastily, without really checking the material. While training your students in critical or information literacy extends beyond the language classroom, you can support the process in two ways:

- Preselect websites to use in internet projects rather than allowing your students to start from scratch and lose valuable time searching for useful material.
- Provide students with tools to evaluate websites. Below is a template you could use to evaluate the appropriateness of resources on the web.

In addition to completing an evaluation form, ask your students to consider the following:

Look at the final group of letters after the dot in the website address, for example, 'com'. This group of letters is the domain, and gives you valuable information about the author of the website. Some common domains are 'com' for 'commercial', 'edu' for 'educational', and 'gov' for 'governmental'. Two-letter domains are country codes, for example 'us' for USA, 'uk' for the UK, 'it' for Italy, 'cz' for Czech Republic, etc.

If you can identify the author or organization, perform an internet search. Can you verify the credentials?

What organizations are linked to the site? What banners (advertisements that appear on websites which viewers can click on) are displayed?

Multimedia literacy

New technologies have opened up multiple avenues to communicate beyond the written word. Today it is possible to communicate with sound, video, text, animation, and **hyperlinks**. But whereas a generation ago we would choose between these different media, today, all the media are converging, and a text may include audio, video, animation, photos and pictures, written text, and hyperlinks. To be literate in such a complex environment requires competence in manipulating the various constituent multimedia elements that make up a new digital text.

↓ COPYRIGHT AND PLAGIARISM

The same copyright law applies to material on the web as to books, magazines, and other published material. But because information is so easy to access on the internet, many students (and teachers) look at copying content from the internet as a trivial offence – somehow different from taking passages from a book. It is as if online material somehow belongs to everybody the moment it is added to the world wide web.

Define your teaching model

Website evaluation form	
Basic information	
Website name/URL	
Is the author identified?	
Date last updated	
Organization and navigation	
Is the site clearly organized?	
Are the links clearly marked?	
Is it easy to move forwards and backwards?	
Are there any broken links (e.g. when you click on a web address do you get an error message)?	
If there is advertising, is any of it invasive or inappropriate?	
Functionality	
Does the site load? Quickly?	
Is there interactivity: can the user do more than just view information?	
Can you contact the publisher?	
Content	
Is the content age-appropriate?	
Is the language level appropriate?	
Is the content verifiable?	
Is the content objective?	
Is the content up-to-date?	
Is the content visually appealing?	
Is there a multimedia element on the site? If so, does it support the content and make it easier to understand?	

FIGURE 1.1 *Website evaluation form*

Photocopiable © Oxford University Press

Define your teaching model

One reason for this is the ease with which one can copy, paste, or download text, images, and audio/video files from the web. There are, however, four very clear rules on copyright which you should discuss with your students and follow yourself.

1 It is fine to link. You can connect your site to another acceptable site on the internet (obviously not sites displaying inappropriate material).

2 Do not take information from a website unless permission is given by the authors. This permission is often stated on the webpage, but in cases where it is not, you should write to the webmaster/author of the site in question and make a formal written request to use the material. Some sites allow use for educational purposes but restrict commercial use.

3 It is permissible to use copyright material for a purpose beyond and/or different from the author's original intention. In other words, if you use a segment from a movie (for example, a trailer) to create a film review, this would be acceptable use of the copyright material ('fair use'). Fair use can also be measured in terms of the amount of material used. Copying an entire text is much less likely to be fair use than copying a short paragraph. This consideration has a lot to do with the financial impact of the use in question. Obviously, if you download a copyrighted text in its entirety, you are taking away from the author's potential market for the material. Fair use is interpreted differently from country to country, so check your local laws to be sure.

4 You are on safest ground when you stick to material which is open to everybody to use – what we call the 'public domain'. Many authors and organizations post their material to the public domain from the start. Other material becomes public domain when its copyright expires. Most websites will explicitly state whether their material is copyrighted. However, when in doubt it is always a good idea to assume that all content is protected. If you wish to use this material contact the website owners. They may have no objection if it is to be used for educational purposes.

There are also organizations which manage public domain material. A good place to start is Creative Commons: http://search.creativecommons.org. Creative Commons awards licences to authors interested in sharing their work with others without complicated copyright restrictions.

There are various levels of licences. Some licences allow for sharing, but forbid commercial use of the materials. Others allow sharing, but not modification of the material. You can search the site for text, images, sound, and video files as well as the type of licence that fits your needs.

Two other sites with public domain material useful in language teaching are:

● Internet Archive
  http://www.archive.org/about/about.php
  This site archives movies, text, audio, software, and digital educational resources. It also has excellent links to many other sites.
● Project Gutenberg
  http://www.gutenberg.org/wiki/Main_Page
  This is the largest collection of free e-books in the world.

Define your teaching model

 *Getting it right*

How to identify plagiarized passages

Some students are very bold about plagiarizing, copying whole sections of text from the web and pasting it into their own work. If you are in any doubt about a segment of text in a student's work, highlight a small section and paste it into a **search engine** such as Google (www.google.com). The search often reveals the passage the material was taken from.

2 Being aware of the issues

The internet can be a dangerous place if you do not pay attention to security. Dangers can range from relatively benign spam (unwanted email) to **viruses** which can cause you to lose all your data. Perhaps more ominous, the anonymous nature of the web allows unscrupulous people to steal your information, or even your identity. Even more alarming, especially for unsuspecting young internet users, is that it allows them to establish friendships over the web without ever meeting the person face-to-face, only to find out later that their 'friend' is a predator. Clearly, internet security needs to be taken very seriously.

The six golden rules of internet security

1 Never share personal information online. The ability to communicate across the world opens up amazing opportunities, but it can also be risky. You can never be one hundred per cent sure who you are talking to when you contact people on the web. In order to protect yourself and your students, never reveal any personal information such as addresses or telephone numbers, and be especially careful about posting photographs to a website. If you conduct class projects with a partner school, check that the information is protected. With school-age children, be sure to get written parental consent for a student's picture to appear on a website. Failure to do so can lead to lawsuits against you and your organization.

2 Install anti-virus software. Viruses are programmes that can potentially harm and even destroy your data. There are many different types of viruses: spyware (which tracks your movements on the web), Trojan horses, and worms. There are a number of subscription anti-virus programmes available on the web which update automatically when you connect to the internet.

3 Create a firewall for your computer. A **firewall** is a programme which blocks access to your computer by unapproved users. Today it is quite common for malicious users to try to 'hack' into computer systems to gain unauthorized access to a computer. The hacker may be doing this for fun or with the aim of stealing or deleting your data. In many cases, hackers take over computers to commit crimes, using an unsuspecting victim's email address to conduct fraud. Most modern operating systems have built-in firewalls. Ensure that they are turned on before you go online. You can do this when you are using a windows-based **operating system** by

opening up the control panel and clicking on the windows firewall icon. Here you can set the level of protection you desire, making exceptions for sites you trust and frequently use.

4 Do not open email attachments from unfamiliar addresses. Many viruses use email attachments to sneak onto your computer. When you open the attachment, the virus is released. Be wary of any email from an unknown sender, especially if the sender addresses you in a very personal way and is trying to raise your interest by adding a subject header that could be of direct interest to you. Be sure to screen the email with your anti-virus software. Even if you know the sender, you should screen all emails as the sender may not be aware they are infected. In some cases the scammer manages to get into address books and infiltrate the email account, sending emails from that person's address.

5 Always log off when you are finished with an online session. The more time you spend unnecessarily connected, the greater the likelihood you may be attacked. Instead of leaving an application running in the background while you do something else, be sure to disconnect.

6 Always back up your data. Nothing is more frustrating than having a computer crash and losing all your data. Play it safe and back up your data regularly, at least once a week. The easiest way to back up data is to save it onto a CD, DVD, or portable USB stick which you can plug into the USB port of your computer. You can also use an external **hard drive** to back up everything on your computer. All you need to do is find the files you want to save and drag and drop them onto the CD, DVD, or USB stick icon. If your institution has a central server, you can back up your computer files there. You can also consider using an online backup service. These services will save your data on their server.

↓ TRAINING

Let's assume you have all the technology you want, purchased and installed effectively. Now you and your colleagues have to learn how to use it. Training is the big hidden cost in technology implementation.

Here are some tips to make training popular and effective:

- Training should be regular and consistent. Develop a training plan for the entire year and stick to it. Like students, teachers want predictability.
- Training should be given in small doses. Technology training does not lend itself to intensive treatment. If you do a one-week intensive pre-service seminar, you can be sure that much of what is learnt will not be retained. Also, teachers are busy people, who need to prepare classes, grade student work, etc. Consider keeping training sessions to under an hour, but hold them frequently.
- Focus on one key point per session. Do not try and cover too much ground in each session. Introduce one tool or application at a time.
- Encourage peer teaching. Rather than teaching technology skills from the top-down, have teachers teach each other. This will build teacher

confidence and promote community-building and resource-sharing. Look for technology champions among your staff who would be willing to serve as trainers.

- Teach skills that teachers can take away and use. Make sure the skills you teach in each session are practical and linked to activities they can use in their classrooms with a minimum of modification.
- Work with the technology companies. If your school has recently bought new technology, get the local company to provide training to your teachers. They should be willing to do this for free or at a minimal cost. They can talk your staff through the more technical aspects of the tools and you can focus on their educational use.
- Try it out yourself first. Before you introduce any technology activities into the classroom, try out the technology tools yourself. Practice makes perfect. Once you feel confident using a tool you are better able to guide your students. Correct a document with track changes, make a PowerPoint presentation, blog, or wiki. Experiment with adding pictures, or even video and audio to a document.

↓ EVALUATING TECHNOLOGY-BASED ACTIVITIES

One way to help you stay on task is to develop a rubric, which is a set of criteria for each of your technology-based activities. In a rubric you create specific criteria for evaluating an activity. You can use these criteria to evaluate your students' work or simply to help you design your activities. By thinking about these criteria you can quickly see which aspects of your activity are language-based and which are focused on the technology alone.

To create a rubric for a web activity it is best to work backwards. Start with the final product of the activity, or if there is no actual product, identify the overall communicative goal. For example, if you assign a PowerPoint project to your students, your criteria might be the following: organization, accuracy, content, and visual appeal. Once you have established your criteria, you can break each one down into specific standards. The specific standards should provide a balance between language and technology goals as illustrated in Table 2.1. Accuracy and content are clearly language driven, whereas visual appeal is a technology/design issue. Organization, on the other hand, relates to both.

Organization	Accuracy	Content	Visual appeal
Slides are in logical order	Correct spelling and pronunciation	Good use of vocabulary	Easy to follow
			Good use of colour
Identifies main ideas and details	Correct use of grammar	Addresses topic	Appropriate use of graphic elements, transitions, and animation
		Creative use of language	

TABLE 2.1 *Evaluation rubric for a Microsoft PowerPoint project*

There are literally thousands of sites on the internet where you can find rubrics you can modify to fit your needs. Many sites actually come with rubric generators which allow you to create your own rubrics with a professional look and feel. See Useful websites (page 93) for more details.

↓ FINAL THOUGHTS ON IMPLEMENTATION

As a final step before implementation, it is important to look closely at your curriculum.

What are your learning goals? Is the learning goal you achieve through technology worth the time invested?

Take a moment to look at your coursebook, if you use one. What are the topics? Are there particular topics which lend themselves to a technology component? Are there certain activities you really don't like and would like to replace?

Most coursebooks try and provide examples of authentic materials to illustrate teaching points. Can you think of ways of using the internet as an alternative means of presentation or as a way of supporting the core topic?

Finally, once you have made your initial choices, be sure to review them at regular intervals. While you can't go out and buy new technology for your entire system every time a new tool comes out, you can test new technologies on a limited scale, in one classroom or on one computer. Encourage the software and/or hardware companies to let you use their products for a free trial period. If their product is good they should be happy to oblige.

 *Getting it right*

Make the most of free software

Many applications that once had to be bought are now available on the internet. A large number of these applications are 'open-source', that is, available free. Before you buy software applications for your computer, check what is available free online. Something out there might just fit your needs and save you a lot of money.

Part 2   Using offline tools

3 Word processing tools

With the internet on everybody's mind, it's easy to forget that not all technology is online. In this section we will look at offline options installed directly on your computer. We will not discuss commercial CD-based language software. Instead we will look at common applications found on most computers and demonstrate how they can be manipulated to support the language learning process.

Of course there are many fine examples of software for language learning. At the back of the book you will find links to software developers and sites which review their products.

↓ WORKING WITH WORD PROCESSORS

Of all today's technologies, word processing is probably the most familiar. Remember typewriters? Well, your students probably don't. If they are under 25, there is a good chance that they have never used one in their life. Word processors are so common nowadays that you probably can't even remember learning to use them. Most of the basic functions such as inserting and deleting, cutting and pasting, highlighting, underlining, and circling you probably don't consciously take note of. But if you think about them a little bit, you will soon realize that they can be used very effectively in the language classroom. Below are a few examples.

Inserting and deleting

Inserting and deleting text on paper is a messy, one-time business. Once a worksheet is filled out, that's it – you can never use it again. Working with a word processing programme allows students to repeat an activity any number of times and to save the results.

Try this ☞ **Insert the spaces**
Type a sentence or short text into a new word processing document and replace the capitals with lower case letters. Then eliminate all the spaces between words, so that you have one long 'word', for example:
wheniwasachildiusedtogotoseemygrandmotheringermany
The students' task is to read the text, insert spaces where appropriate, and add correct punctuation:
When I was a child, I used to go and see my grandmother in Germany.
Students can save and print their improved texts and check for accuracy with classmates.

Try this ☞   **Collaborative stories**

To make up collaborative stories, you start off with a sentence on the board, for example, *An old man sat by the side of the road.* Each student opens a Word document and types in this sentence, and then writes a follow-up sentence in their document. They then move onto the next computer, where they now add a new sentence to their classmate's document. They continue in this way until they are back at their original computers. Each student can then read their story and work in pairs to edit the stories they have on their screen.

Cut and paste

The ability to move chunks of text quickly within a document (and to retrace your steps if you make an error) is a great asset in the editing process.

Try this ☞   **Sentence sequencing**

Type a short text into a document. Then cut and paste the individual sentences in jumbled order. Students read the mixed-up text and use the cut and paste function to put the text in the appropriate order. Alternatively, the students can create texts of their own and challenge their classmates to reorder them.

Track changes

As the name suggests, when you work on a document with track changes turned on, any insertions, deletions, or formatting changes you make to a text are tracked for you to review. You can customize the appearance of the changes you make but the most common choice is for insertions to appear underlined and in colour in the body of the text, while deletions and formatting changes appear in bubbles in the right margin with a dotted line to the relevant point in the document. Track changes also allow you to make comments linked to points in the text. These comments appear in bubbles in the right margin (see Screenshot 3.1).

When using track changes it is important to bear in mind that you must choose to accept or reject changes before they are permanently integrated into a document. You can review each change individually or simply click 'accept all changes' if you agree to them all.

Track changes provides a number of options for customizing editing. You can choose to view the original document and the edited version both with and without changes. It is also possible to have multiple reviewers propose edits or make comments. It is possible to display all these changes together, or you can choose to look at each reviewer's changes individually, which is useful since multiple reviewer changes can be hard to follow.

Word processing tools

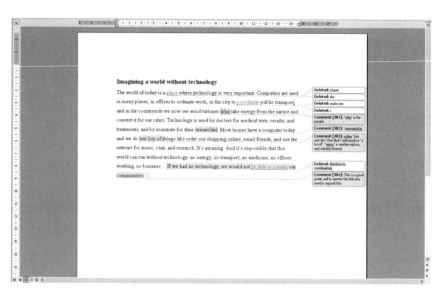

SCREENSHOT 3.1   *Track changes*

Track changes is extremely useful for correcting student work. It enables you to create an electronic dialogue with the writer, which emphasizes the writing process and not just the end product. Track changes is also useful for students working on group tasks. The possibility for multiple reviewers to edit a document allows all members of a group to participate equally. Track changes can also help individual students write more freely since they experiment with a text before committing to a final version.

For more specific information on how to use track changes, refer to the link to Microsoft online training at the back of this book. Of course, there are also many other tutorials online to choose from as well.

✓ *Getting it right*

How to finalize documents in track changes

When you are ready to finalize the document you are working on, you must accept or reject the changes you have made, using the dropdown on the tick button or the cross button (found on the **toolbar**). Only then will the changes you have tracked disappear.

Highlighting, circling, and underlining

Word processing programmes provide students and teachers with a number of tools which can be quite useful for identifying and/or isolating parts of a text. Below are some examples.

Try this  **Highlighting parts of speech**

The highlight function can be used to raise your students' grammar awareness. Give them a text and ask them to highlight certain parts of speech, say, phrasal verbs, or adjectives. Since it is easy to change between highlight colours, you can colour code for parts of speech, for example:

red = nouns
blue = adjectives
green = verbs
yellow = prepositions
pink = phrasal verbs

Students can then check each other's work on-screen.

As an alternative to highlighting, you could use font colour, bold, italic, and underline for parts of speech (these functions can be found in the toolbar at the top of a word processing screen). This option is useful if you want your students to print out their work for comparison and correction.

Try this

Reading comprehension

The highlight, bold, italic, and underline functions can also be useful for supporting critical reading, especially at higher levels. For example, students can use bold for main idea and topic sentences; italicize linking words; underline key details; and highlight important facts (with different colours depending on importance).

One disadvantage of word processing is that, as documents look very professional, it is easy to see them as more polished than they might actually be, in terms of both content and accuracy. Students may tend to regard their first draft as final because it looks good, without revising and improving the content.

✓ *Getting it right*

How to find your way round printed text

When working with a long text which does not fit onto one page, students can lose their place **scrolling** through the text in print layout. To make it easier, use the reading layout, which takes you from one page to the next, more like reading a book. Layouts are found under 'View' on the toolbar.

PowerPoint and other presentation software

Microsoft PowerPoint is an excellent entry point into the world of multimedia tools. It's like a sophisticated OHT in some ways. It is a highly flexible tool based on simple templates that allow students with little background knowledge to create professional-looking presentations. PowerPoint slides can include images, sound, animation, and video. They can also be linked to outside resources or linked internally, creating the feeling of having a homepage and sub-pages, rather than a linear progression.

PowerPoint activities promote both oral and written language. Students can create slides to support a verbal presentation or simply use the slides as 'pages in a book'.

PowerPoint presentations are an equally useful presentation tool for you, the teacher. With PowerPoint you can introduce key concepts to your class, integrating words, pictures, and sound to give them a rich multimedia

Word processing tools

experience that supports (scaffolds) their understanding. This is very helpful if you have a large or mixed-ability class.

While PowerPoint offers users a variety of layouts and formatting options, all choices are governed by the space of each individual slide. The requirement to write within a defined space is of great benefit in the language classroom. The writer has to learn to be precise and economical in deciding what to include.

Students must also evaluate and prioritize information and create cohesion between individual slides. This supports core academic skills such as identifying a main idea and supporting details. PowerPoint can serve as a useful planning tool in preparing academic writing tasks.

Organization of slides is made very easy through the slide sorter function of PowerPoint. The slide sorter displays all the slides in a presentation and allows the writer to change the order of slides by dragging them to a new position. Students can experiment and brainstorm and reorganize their presentation as they go along. Using the slide sorter function is a lot like using index cards to organize a talk or text. However, with PowerPoint, in one single process, the user can reorganize and edit the content of each slide.

PowerPoint presentations also promote differentiation in the classroom. Some students may use the slides to support an oral presentation. They may be very simple and sparse references, designed as much to keep the speaker on track as to inspire the audience, especially if the speaker has a tendency to move about the classroom. Other students may choose very elaborate graphics and make the presentation a highly visual experience that may or may not be accompanied by a student narrative. Some students who are perhaps shy when speaking publicly, may choose to pre-record their voice to accompany the slides. There are even programmes, such as Captivate or Breeze, which allow students to turn their PowerPoints into small narrated flash movies.

✔ *Getting it right*

Helping students produce good presentations

Presentation software has lots of functions, so some rules for your students can be helpful:

1 Give your students a limit to the number of slides they can include, and tell them to use the first slide for the title of the presentation, their name, and the date.
2 Decide together on a font that is easy to read, and show the class how dark fonts on light backgrounds work better from a distance.
3 Tell your students to avoid long sentences or too many points per slide.
4 Tell your students to limit the use of special effects, such as fading, blinking, and spinning, which can be annoying if used excessively.

✔ *Getting it right*

Plan presentations on paper first

Encourage your students to plan their slides on paper before they prepare their presentation on the computer. You may want to create a wireframe (a photocopiable template of empty boxes) to give to your students for their planning.

Some PowerPoint activities

Below are a few sample PowerPoint ideas which illustrate how distinct language tasks can be woven into the presentation process. It is important to keep these language goals firmly in mind when designing activities. After all, our goal is language and not IT skill development!

Try this ☞ **Ideal city**

In this activity your students act as city planners, with the power to change anything they want about their city. You can do this by brainstorming with your class the things they like and dislike about their home city and the services provided such as recreation, power, transportation, schools, etc. The students work in small groups and make a PowerPoint presentation of their plans for an ideal city, creating their own drawings or using images they find on the web to illustrate their slides. They should map out their ideas on paper before using the computers. When they have finished, you can either save the slides on a USB stick or ask students to upload them onto a class website or wiki (see page 65).

Try this ☞ **Talking books**

For this activity, you need to have 20–30 digital photos of objects, people, and places uploaded onto your students' computers for them to use in class. You can do this by saving them into a file under 'My Pictures' on the computers, using one computer per group of four to six students. Your students' task is to work in small groups using six to eight of the pictures to create a story. They then make a presentation, but instead of writing the story on the slides, they tell the story, with pictures supporting what they say. When the students have completed their presentations and texts, supply a small microphone and have each group record their texts. It is really easy to do. Simply go to the slide in question, click 'Insert menu > Movies and sounds > Record sound'. A recorder will appear. Be sure all the students get a chance to speak at least for one slide each. If you like, let the students add sound effects.

PowerPoint games

It is very easy to create games, using PowerPoint's linking function. Any object (a picture or text) can be linked to another slide in a PowerPoint presentation. This makes it possible, for example, to create a 'Jeopardy'-style trivia board game (www.jeopardy.com), with columns of boxes where students click on a hidden hyperlink, and are led to a second slide with a question and set of answers. The answers are then hyperlinked to other slides (for example: 'That's right!' Or 'Try again!'). Using the same linking principle you can also create a board game where each space is hyperlinked to a forfeit or any other task you may choose (see Table 3.1).

There are numerous online tutorials that explain step by step the process of creating PowerPoint games. Many contain templates where all you have to do is enter the relevant content. Some good examples of websites with lots of tutorials are listed in Useful websites at the end of this book.

Word processing tools

Food vocabulary	The past	Phrasal verbs	Prepositions	Question tags	The future
€100	€100	€100	€100	€100	€100
€200	€200	€200	€200	€200	€200
€300	€300	€300	€300	€300	€300
€400	€400	€400	€400	€400	€400
€500	€500	€500	€500	€500	€500

TABLE 3.1   *Jeopardy game*

4   Interactive whiteboards

Interactive whiteboards are exciting tools that have quickly spread to classrooms across the globe. Everyone seems to have heard of them, but many people are not entirely clear about what they are and what they really do. Before we move forward then, a definition is in order.

An IWB is a touch-sensitive board that is connected to a computer and a projector (and other peripherals such as DVD players if necessary) and displays a computer desktop. Unlike a conventional projector, it allows the computer to be controlled by touching the projection on the board. In some ways, IWBs are very much like PowerPoint programmes with touch screens and additional interactive features.

IWBs are excellent examples of seamless technology – tools that allow us to run multiple media from one place. Even a novice user can take advantage of this. It is truly a multimedia tool, allowing the teacher (and student) to toggle (switch) easily between applications. You can work on a document and quickly jump to the internet for a reference or play a video from the web or the DVD drive on your computer. Working with an IWB instead of using a mouse and keyboard, keeps your eyes up and your focus on your students rather than on your computer.

Understanding IWBs

Interactive whiteboards are best understood as three components:

1 the board itself
2 the software that comes with it
3 software produced for the IWB by publishers.

Interactive whiteboards are not **plug and play** tools, which you can start using the moment you connect them to your computer. You need to learn each IWB's functionality and this requires a lot of hands-on training. The more you train, the more interactive the board gets.

IWB software tools

Each IWB comes with its own set of software tools which you and your students can use to edit content on the whiteboard. These tools are very similar to the editing tools you might find in a word processing programme like Microsoft Word. They can be used to create text with multiple fonts

Interactive whiteboards

and colours, and to add shapes, lines, and boxes. But in addition to these practical tools IWBs come with additional functionality. While each software package does differ, here are a few functions most IWBs share:

- Spotlighting: the board is blacked out except for a small spotlight which you can move and increase and decrease in size. This is useful for prediction activities.
- Drag and drop: you can create text or pictures, select them and drag and drop them anywhere on the screen. This is arguably the hardest kind of function to recreate in the classroom without an IWB and a computer.
- Hide/reveal: with this function you can hide all or part of the screen and slowly reveal it, either from left to right and right to left or top to bottom and bottom to top. This function is very valuable when checking comprehension, going over exercises or, as with the spotlight tool, doing prediction activities.

While the text tools may not be unique to IWB software, their application is very different. Whereas a text tool in Microsoft Word will allow you to edit a document in that specific programme, IWB software allows you to edit and annotate anything on your computer screen. Rather than just using the pen to 'click open' applications, it is possible to write over the top of applications such as videos, word documents, or PowerPoint presentations and save these annotated documents as separate files.

If you edit a document, you probably want to save it; IWB software allows you to do just that. This can be incredibly helpful if you run out of time and have work on the board you would like to keep to use another time.

IWB software also makes it possible to create your own IWB files, often referred to as flipcharts. These flipcharts can serve as lesson plans for your class and can include links to any media available on or through your class computer. These flipcharts can consist of multiple sheets. You can save a default copy of these sheets for your files, so that you always have a record of what you did in class. You can also mark up other versions as much as you like: simply save these versions using a different name. Instantly you have a set of records of your lesson as used with different classes.

 *Getting it right*

Practise writing on an IWB before using it in class

Writing with an IWB pen feels different at first from writing with a board marker, so take time to get used to it. It's also good to familiarize yourself with the board pen(s) and some of their functions, such as highlighting, underlining, circling, colouring in, and so on.

Publisher software for the IWB

More and more publishers are developing IWB versions of popular coursebook series. The IWB versions are CD-based and designed to work with most IWB systems. After starting the programme you will see a menu screen where you can choose what unit and/or specific activities you would like to work with (see Screenshot 4.2).

SCREENSHOT 4.1   *Main menu and submenu, Solutions iTools, Oxford University Press*

Publisher software makes working with the IWB easy. The software contains games, audio and video clips, and digital pages from the coursebook and workbook. What were once all individual items are now found in one place in the IWB software. The IWB coursebook brings the page alive and, as with any other programme on the IWB, you can edit it and save the lesson as a separate file.

✓ *Getting it right*

Use printed materials alongside the IWB

IWB software is designed to be used in conjunction with traditional printed materials. Students like to have books and will want to be able to take them home and refer to them. We can't assume that students and teachers are ready to go one hundred per cent digital!

Making the IWB interactive

One of the criticisms of interactive whiteboards is that they are not particularly interactive. In many classrooms students are focused on the screen in audience mode. This way of using the IWB is of value, but it leaves out a crucial element – the power of the pen. When the pen is handed over to the students, the power of the board is revealed.

If one regards a lesson as something involving a mixture of individual, pair, group, and whole-class work, there may well be far more ways to integrate the IWB than at first appears. Interactivity may be an issue not only of physical manipulation, but of increased attention and focus. Seen this way, IWBs can turn individual tasks performed on computer consoles into whole-group activities. If we really try and integrate technology into the overall lesson plan, we have a number of options for using the board:

- Use the board to give instructions and provide examples. Rather than handing out directions or writing steps on the board, use the whiteboard to go over the steps with the entire class. In doing so you can link each step to a concrete example of the product or invite students to the board to demonstrate a process.
- Brainstorm with the entire class.

- Have the class complete a project on individual computers and display their results via the whiteboard to the entire class.
- Invite students to the front and allow them to write on the board, creating a text or annotating their colleagues' work.
- Invite groups of students to the board to solve a problem.

The sheer size of the IWB makes it easier for certain students to work in groups on-screen, while providing the rest of the class with something to follow. This keeps everyone involved.

Interactive whiteboards are multi-sensory and this appeals to various learning styles. It is visual, oral, and through the pen, even physical. Interactive whiteboards are not cheap, but they are an interesting alternative in situations where individual computers may be too bulky to fit in the classroom.

Choosing an IWB

Interactive whiteboards are a major investment. There are many options to choose from and each one has pluses and minuses, depending on your circumstances. In many cases, your organization will make the choice for you, but if you are still in the planning phase consider the following points:

- Mobility: some whiteboard systems require dedicated whiteboards which are themselves interactive, while other systems can scan any surface and make it interactive. Fixed dedicated whiteboards have the advantage of stability. The interactivity is in the board itself. Non-fixed systems need to be calibrated each time they are used. However, these systems are decidedly cheaper than fixed board solutions.
- Support networks: most IWB manufacturers have resource websites with links to lesson plans created for the interactive whiteboard and tutorials to help you get the most out of this technology. Compare resource sites of major IWB producers before you finalize your choice.

Try this ☞ **Spotlighting**

Choose a photograph or picture that supports the language you are learning in class. This could be vocabulary you have studied or a description of a scene (for example a still-life painting or a street scene). You may want to introduce multiple images beforehand, as you would do if you were using flashcards in an activity. Focus the spotlight on one section of the screen and allow the students to guess: *Is it ...?* or *It's ...* . If the students are unable to guess correctly, slowly increase the size of the spotlight or simply move the spotlight to another part of the screen. Then invite students to the front to choose an image and control the spotlight.

Note: you can also do spotlighting using video.

Some other simple and effective activities using the IWB's applications are:

Try this ☞ **Categorizing**

Create columns in the centre of an empty whiteboard screen. This can be done by using the table tool or simply drawing columns with the electronic pen. The columns could be vocabulary categories (food, animals, activities), grammatical structures (verbs versus nouns, various tenses), or sound categories (/z/ versus /s/). Position words and images to the side of the columns. Students then click on each word or picture and drag it into the appropriate column.

For more advanced students, type words randomly onto an empty whiteboard and invite students to the board to reorganize and classify them in a logical fashion. This can also be done as a graphic organizer activity with students creating mind maps linking ideas and concepts.

Try this ☞ **Story or sentence scramble**

Align pictures and/or words in jumbled order and invite students to move the objects around into an appropriate order. If you are working with images, you can also ask the students to write a sentence corresponding to each picture.

Try this ☞ **Grammar explanation**

Create empty diagrams and drag and drop examples into these diagrams as you explain (see Screenshot 4.2). Alternatively, invite students to drag and drop the correct information to complete the diagram.

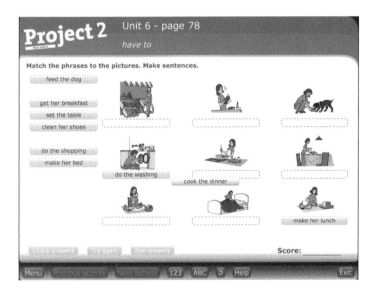

SCREENSHOT 4.2   *Drag and drop exercise, Solutions iTools, Oxford University Press*

Try this ☞ **Labelling**

Draw or import a picture and position some text below or to the side of it. Students then drag the text to the appropriate place on the picture.

Try this ☞ **Hide and reveal**

Use 'hide and reveal' to introduce and practise grammatical structures, such as the present perfect (see Screenshot 2.4). In one column write the subject pronouns and in a second column write the correct present perfect of a verb, for example *have spoken, has spoken*. Either cover up the right-hand column and slowly reveal from left to right, or move from the top to the bottom and have students predict the next line in the diagram.

Interactive whiteboards

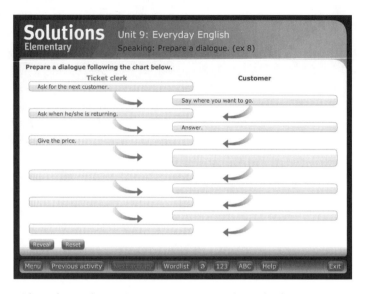

SCREENSHOT 4.3   *Hide and reveal exercise using Project iTools, Oxford University Press*

Part 3   Using online tools

5

Email, chats, and text messaging

Email

Email presents interesting writing challenges. Email lies somewhere between written and oral language. It is less formal than a letter, but certainly more structured than a chat contribution or a text message. Emails should be kept short. If you want to send a long message, include it as an attachment, where it is less likely to get corrupted – do not put it in the body of an email.

Email is an asynchronous tool (partners do not have to be online at the same time to communicate). This has certain distinct advantages over chat, which is a synchronous written communication tool (communication takes place in real time, like spoken communication). Chat requires a higher degree of fluency to be effective, and can be a huge challenge to lower-level language learners. In addition, email communication is easier to organize for teachers. Since there is no need to arrange a specific time to be online to communicate with a partner, email projects can be flexibly scheduled and even conducted from one computer if necessary.

Since its development for commercial use in the 1980s, email has been a popular form of communication used to establish contacts, often known as twinning, with partner schools or learners around the world. With email you can address both individuals and groups and you can add attachments to your mail to share with your partners.

Now that there are more flexible online tools in the form of wikis and social networks (see page 75), the role of email in twinning projects may diminish. Working on twinning projects via email is always an individual experience, whether the mail is sent to a group or one student. The documents are not anchored in any shared space. With wikis and social networks, the collaborative work facility is centralized. The participants in a project are pulled to the wiki site to access information and edit. It acts like a magnet, drawing students in, unlike email which distributes information, and pushes it out.

Below is an example of a possible email project. Later on, when we discuss wikis, we can return to this example and see if email is the best format for it.

Try this ☞ **Same life, different location**

In this project, students link with a corresponding school in another country. The school may be in an English-speaking country or, as an interesting alternative, it could involve schools from two non English-speaking countries communicating through the medium of English – something that is becoming more and more common these days. The goal of the project is to compare the lives of students and reflect on the similarities and differences they find.

This project can be carried out on a number of different levels. Some points to compare are:

• daily schedules
• subjects studied
• living spaces
• popular culture
• free time.

Each student can choose one aspect of life to work on and then exchange documents with a partner from the corresponding school. As a final step, students can write a paragraph outlining how their life would change if they were to trade places.

Try this ☞ **Story circles**

Before class, make a numbered list of your students. Write the first sentence of a story, for example *Sarah didn't go to school on Friday*, in the body of an email and send it to the first student on the list. This student writes the next sentence in the story and then forwards the email to the next student on the list and so on, until every student has had a chance to write a sentence. End after one round or, if the students are still interested, continue with another round. Print out the story and hand a copy to your students. In pairs, have the students edit the story for language errors. Finally, go over the errors with the class.

If you have established contacts with partners in another school or country, you could also extend the circle to make it international.

Dialogue journals

Dialogue journals are essentially written conversations between two people. Email is a particularly useful medium for setting up dialogue journals. Observations have shown that because email is less governed by rules of style, students tend to write more than in conventional paper-and-pencil tasks. Also, because email can be restricted to a very limited audience (as little as one), it is a safe place for students to practise and gain confidence before moving onto a more public forum, such as a blog or wiki (see page 63).

Dialogue journals between student and teacher generally begin with a question. When starting out with dialogue journals, make the question very concrete, for example, *What's your favourite food?* You then comment on the response and add a follow-up or introduce a new topic. Once the students feel confident responding, you can have the student choose a topic. Another option is to use the dialogue journal as a feedback element on class materials or teaching.

Chat

Chatting is a synchronous activity: at least two people must be online simultaneously in order to chat. Chats take place in chat rooms, where online users gather to interact. Traditionally, chats were text-based: essentially, you read messages by other users in the same room and respond.

Chat rooms are organized according to various criteria: common interest (sports, language learning, technology), age, or geographical location. Most web browsers (Yahoo!, MSN, Google) come with their own built-in chat programmes. Many websites have built-in chat functionality as well.

While the great majority of chats are still text-based, there is also a fast-growing number that also offer voice and/or video communication – Skype (www.skype.com) and Yahoo! Messenger (www.yahoo.com) being the most best known examples. These multimedia chats allow students to use all the options at once. They do not have to toggle between text, sound, and video. They can listen via headphones, speak into a microphone, watch the webcam, and read the text chat all at the same time.

As mentioned earlier, synchronous communication can be difficult for language learners. It makes little sense to have your students spend lots of time online simply thinking before typing a response to a post. However, voice and video chats relieve students of the burden of writing and allow for real spoken communication across countries and continents.

While chatting can be challenging for lower-level students, it has great potential for students at a higher level. The fact that they can use voice, video, and text makes it possible to integrate skills in one place at one time quite naturally. Students can listen to an opinion, read a text comment, write a reply, and speak to a fellow student all in real time.

Below are some straightforward activities using chats.

Try this ☞ **Text chat brainstorm**

Use text chat to moderate a brainstorming session when introducing a topic, for example for 'global social awareness' you might use text chat to brainstorm 'different uses of water'. The advantage of using text chat is that you can actually capture the transcript and save the thinking process.

Try this ☞ **Debates**

Even the most reluctant student has an opinion about something. Brainstorm debate topics with your class and agree on one to follow up in an online debate. To make it more exciting, you can invite students from other classes (or even another school) to join you in an online debate at a mutually convenient time. Before the debate, email a list of those students who are going to debate 'for' and who are going to debate 'against' the motion, so that on the day it is clear who is doing what. Prepare some key words and phrases that your students might need, and go through these in class before the online debate. Make sure that your debate has a clear end time, and that you are on hand to intervene if either side of the debate runs out of ideas or the debate starts going off track.

Try this ☞ Project work

Chats can be useful to promote groupwork when group members are not at the same location. You can email a file to all group members and talk or write about it in real time. If you have your files on a wiki, you can even make changes as you go along.

Try this ☞ Radio plays

Students collaborate online and write a script for a radio play. During the course of a series of voice-chat sessions (which could be in class time), the actors can practise their show and then invite a broader audience to the final performance, all online.

Try this ☞ Online question time with your twinned school

Chat is an excellent opportunity for students in twinned schools to conduct a 'live interview' with their counterpart. Each student will need an internet connection, headphones, and a microphone for this activity. To prepare, agree on a theme such as 'my daily routine', with your counterpart teacher in the twinned school, and twin up each of your students with one of theirs, so that it is clear who is calling who. In class, your students prepare ten core questions for their interviewee on the chosen topic, and prepare to answer questions from their counterparts on the same theme. Their task is to find as many differences between their twin's daily routine and their own.

Text messaging

Text messaging, or texting is really a new language, with abbreviations and rules of its own. This poses a great challenge to teachers. To some, texting is destroying the English language. Clearly, we want to make language learning relevant to students and in this sense texting can't be ignored. Here are two ways you can preserve the English language and still integrate texting into your class.

Try this ☞ Translate texts

Make a list of common text message abbreviations and ask students to 'translate' them. For example:

LOL	laugh out loud/lots of love
CU	see you
BBL	be back later
B4	before
2MORO	tomorrow
CLD	could
BTW	by the way
FYI	for your information

Then ask your students to tell you the abbreviations they use for you to guess.

Emoticons

Emoticons are the funny little pictures students use to express emotions. For example:

:D (laughing), ☹ (unhappy), >:- (angry)

Try this ☞ **Using emoticons**

Ask your students first to identify what each emoticon symbolizes and then to create their own. If you then ask them to explain how you create emoticons from text, this will help them to practise words for punctuation.

6   The world wide web

Have you ever stopped to ask yourself what the world wide web is? To most people, the www and the internet are synonymous, but this is not the case. The internet is a huge **network** of connected computers, linked across the world. The **world wide web** (www) is the part of the internet where information can be accessed. It's the colourful, fun part of the internet, consisting of a limitless and ever-expanding number of pages which we navigate by using web browsers such as Internet Explorer, Mozilla, Netscape, Safari, or Google's Chrome.

Email is on the internet, but is not part of the www. It is a means of communicating rather than accessing information.

Besides being fun, what are the advantages of using the world wide web in our classrooms? Here are a few that come to mind:

- The internet provides authentic content: students and teachers get limitless 'real' content in the target language. They can read a real menu, find out when a train leaves Paddington station, listen to a sports broadcast, or watch a movie trailer. The internet can complement your coursebook by bringing language learning to life. Let's not forget that the internet also provides teachers with lesson plans, ideas banks, test generators, and pretty much anything else you would want to know as a teacher.
- The internet offers meaningful language. Studies have shown that students learn language better when the language they are exposed to is meaningful. The internet creates contexts for language use which, through their authenticity, become purposeful in the eyes of the students. The students actively manipulate the language for a clear and logical purpose.
- The internet promotes critical thinking skills and 'constructivist' learning. On the internet, knowledge is transient. Unlike coursebooks which transmit information in a predictable order, working with the internet is constantly evolving. Students make choices and 'construct' knowledge every time they go online. Each search is unique.
- The internet reduces focus on the teacher. Working with the internet can take the focus off you and shift communication from teacher–student to student–student. If you are a bit unsure of your own English-language skills, authentic listening and reading from the internet can help model the language you want to teach.

- Internet-based work can increase motivation. It is colourful, exciting, and undeniably 'cool'. Computers and the internet are a key component of youth culture and lend language learning street-credibility.

↓ SEARCHING THE WEB

Web browsers

Web browsers are your door to the world wide web. Essentially, web browsers read html code they receive from a website. This code tells the browser how to display information on your computer. You can think of a web browser as a little TV that gets signals from a broadcasting station. Like a TV, each web browser reads this 'signal' slightly differently, so websites may not appear exactly the same in each browser.

In the early days of the world wide web, most information was either text or simple images (photographs or drawings). However, today the web is full of multimedia: audio files, video, and animation formats. Not all web browsers have the software to display every format. When a web browser comes across a format it can't display, it automatically looks for a little programme called a **plug-in**. If you have this plug-in on your computer, it will immediately open it and display the requested content. If it isn't available on your computer, you will need to download the plug-in from the world wide web.

Typical plug-ins you should be sure you have installed on your computer:

- Mediaplayers (such as realplayer, windows media player, or **QuickTime**): these allow you to play video and audio files.
- Adobe Acrobat: this allows you to display documents formatted as **PDFs** (files which can be read without a word processing programme).
- **Flash** and Shockwave: these allow you to open web animation files.
- **Java** (a programming language which can be used across multiple computer platforms, making it very practical for the internet). Applets (mini-programmes that can be used on web pages to make the page fun and interactive) are programmed in Java.

Currently, there are a number of web browsers available to download free from the world wide web. By far the most popular browser is Microsoft's Internet Explorer, which is pre-installed on all Windows-based computers. For Apple Mac computer users there is Safari.

Choosing a web browser is a matter of personal preference. While there are differences, for normal computing needs any of the popular options will provide all the functionality you need.

 **Getting it right**

Avoiding bugs in software

Avoid installing the very latest version of any software until it has been available for at least a year. New software releases often have bugs (errors in programming code) which are only discovered once they are released.

The world wide web

Search engines

If a web browser is your gateway to the internet, a search engine is your guide to its contents. Certainly, if you were to know the **URL** (web address) of each site you wanted to visit, there would be no need for you to use a search engine, but this is like saying that you know exactly which books you want to look for in a library, and this library (the world wide web) contains an unfathomable 100 million websites and 85 billion individual webpages.

In order to help people find their way around the internet, programmers created search engines, websites which allow you to search the web by typing in queries. The most famous of these search engines is undoubtedly Google. In fact, Google is so common in today's world that 'to google' has become a common verb in English – and in many other languages as well. However, Google isn't the only search engine available to you. There are many other popular options such as Yahoo!, or search engines geared towards a specific type of content, such as children's websites, business sites, people-searching sites, job sites, and, of course, sites defined by language or geography.

Search engines do not need to be downloaded. They are websites in themselves. You may also find Google search fields on third party websites as well.

The internet is a non-linear environment where information is accessed according to multiple equal criteria, instead of looking through a hierarchical catalogue. How you search will largely be dependent on your own knowledge and understanding of how information is linked. The search engine tries to interpret your intentions and deliver a set of results based on this logic. Sometimes the results yield immediate benefits, but more often than not, the results will need to be refined.

 *Getting it right*

Use the right tool for searching

Think about what tool you will use when you search. Many people lump search engines like Google and sites like Yahoo! together. They are actually very different. Yahoo! is a search directory where sites are organized into categories. If you know what you are looking for, search directories can save time, much like looking through a telephone book.

Don't forget, not all information contained in a website is known to your search engine. A first search will lead to follow up sub-searches. You may look at the search results and decide to visit a particular website. This website may in turn have links to other sites not listed in your initial search query. You may follow one of these links and soon you will find yourself very far away from the search results page you first started with.

Luckily, your web browser has a very useful function called history. History lists all the websites you have visited during an online session. So, if you find yourself completely lost, you can find your way back.

The world wide web

 *Getting it right*

How to search the web

There is no correct way to search the web but here are two ways of making your searches more effective:

1 Be as precise as possible, since general terms in a search return numerous and general answers.

2 Narrow down a search on a search engine by using **Boolean operators** (words like 'and', 'or', and 'not'). You need to put your search terms in double quotation marks, for example "grammar" and "efl". Using AND always limits results; using OR broadens the results; and using NOT excludes some results.

Getting organized

The resources of the internet are wonderful, but will not be of much use if you can't find them. Although 'history' is useful, it really doesn't help you remember what sites were valuable, or even what they contained for that matter. As a result you can end up jumping from one site to another looking for material without really exploring what is actually available. This is a waste of time.

With so much information available on the web, it is very important to keep all your valuable resources organized. Otherwise you may discover a great nugget of material and never find it again. Searching the internet is dynamic and constantly changing depending on an individual's interests and understanding of how things relate. Web searching is often spontaneous and a minor change in a search request can lead you past the information you are looking for.

Bookmarking

For this reason it is very important to bookmark sites that are relevant to you. Bookmarks (also known as favourites) are websites that you ask your web browser to remember. This is normally done by clicking on the 'favourites' tab and selecting the 'add favourite' command.

Unfortunately, although bookmarking can be a good memory aid, it can also become addictive. Very soon you may find yourself with an enormous unorganized list of websites you have picked up while browsing the web. In many cases you can't even remember why you chose to bookmark the sites in the first place. Luckily, the bookmarks feature also allows you to organize your bookmarks into folders, exactly like the folder structure you use to organize other documents on your computer.

It is very important to think about how you want to structure your data before you begin actively bookmarking. Decide on a hierarchy of information. If your course is thematic, the topic may be the top level of the folder structure. You could also choose to bookmark by skill, grammar point, or level. With so much multimedia on the web it is also very useful to group resources by media type: audio, video, image, text, etc. See if you can come up with a taxonomy that fits your needs (a taxonomy is a system of classifying information into logical categories and sub-categories). Don't worry if the taxonomy isn't perfect. Once you have added a basic structure to your bookmarks, you can change it again at any time by using the 'edit bookmarks' function on your browser to move web links or move and/or create folders. The key is to create a taxonomy that is simple and easy to use.

To practise organizing your bookmarks, you can follow this procedure:

• Open a search engine and search for two or three websites that you particularly like or that interest you.
• Bookmark the sites (add them to your favourites), then create two folders by clicking on the favourites menu.
• Click 'organize favourites'/'create folders'.
• Name the folders to reflect the content of the websites you selected.
• Select one of the websites you added, by left-clicking on the title with your mouse.
• While still holding down the mouse drag the favourite to one of the folders you created and release the mouse.
• Do the same for the other favourites you created.
• If you like, open one of the folders, select a link as above and drag it from its current folder to another folder on your favourites list. In this way you can reorganize your favourites according to your needs.

Try this ☞   **Developing a taxonomy (classifying)**

This is an excellent activity to do with the entire class via the IWB. Using a finger or the electronic pen, students can create a visual representation of the taxonomy in the form of an easily edited mind map which, like a simple file, can be saved to their computer for use another day.

Social bookmarking

Classic bookmarking is helpful, but it has its limitations. Many websites contain information on a number of different subjects that may be relevant to your work. It can be hard to organize them into folders. It is easier if you classify these web links according to multiple criteria. The technology of social bookmarking offers this alternative.

Social bookmarking is built around the concept of tagging. Tagging is a way of attaching key words to a website to help you find it again. Most search engines are based on some form of tagging where the search engine interprets your search based on a scan on the website content. In the case of social bookmarking, you set the tags yourself. Tagging allows you to customize the way your bookmarks are organized, and most importantly, allows you to organize these bookmarks according to equal multiple criteria rather than the hierarchical organization by folders. Organization is important here too. The more uniformly you tag, the more likely it is that you will get each relevant site.

Another key distinction between social and traditional bookmarking is that social bookmarking is based on the internet rather than on your computer. Traditional bookmarks are hosted on your computer in your browser and

The world wide web

can't be shared. Social bookmarks are kept on a bookmarking website and are accessible to anyone who visits the site. Social bookmarking enables you to access your bookmarks whenever you are on a computer with an internet connection, whether it is your computer or not. This can be a very convenient factor if you don't have your own computer to use at work.

In order to create social bookmarks, you need to join a social bookmarking website. The most popular social bookmarking website is known as de.licio.us.com. (see Screenshot 6.1)

SCREENSHOT 6.1   *De.licio.us screen*

Once you join the website, you can create a button that will appear in the toolbar of your browser. Each time you see a website you want to bookmark, you click on this button to add the bookmark to your collection. You tag it by putting your key words in the dialogue box which appears with the name of the link.

You can create an account with a social bookmarking website, where your bookmarks or favourites will automatically be imported. When you choose a bookmark and click 'edit', you will see a tag field, where you can enter tags for this link. To make tagging more precise, you can:

- browse existing tags
- separate tags by spaces
- combine general tags, such as EFL, with more specific criteria such as language level (A1), language point (present perfect), and age group (teenagers).

RSS feeds

RSS feeds are another great way to help you keep up with the ever-changing content on the internet. You've probably seen the symbol for RSS on lots of sites you visit regularly.

FIGURE 6.1   *RSS symbol*

RSS stands for 'really simple syndication'. This means that you can sign up to a site with RSS and receive all new updates to that site delivered directly to you, instead of you having to log onto each site individually and search for what is new. RSS feeds bring the information to you, allowing you to keep up-to-date effortlessly.

In order to access RSS content, you need to sign up for a **reader** which collects the content from multiple websites and displays it on one site, just for you (see Screenshot 6.2). These readers are known as **aggregators** and most are available free on the internet.

SCREENSHOT 6.2   *RSS feeds on an aggregator page*

For advanced students of English, RSS feeds offer an excellent opportunity to individualize content, promote autonomous learning, and provide opportunities for extensive reading.

Once you have logged on, you can add subscriptions to websites by pasting the feed URLs directly into your reader (look for a button that says 'add subscriptions'). However, it is easier to add subscriptions from the selected sites themselves. Nowadays most serious bloggers as well as magazines, newspapers, and other media have buttons linking to RSS feeds. If you click on the button a set of icons appears with names of readers. Click your reader's icon and the RSS feed is set up in your reader. This makes it easy to add feeds as you surf the web – but be careful not to create complete chaos! Organize your feeds into folders and think twice before adding a link. Is it something you will read every day? Your reader will also have numerous settings you can use to control how your feeds appear. Explore them once you feel comfortable with the general functions.

↓ INTERNET SEARCH-BASED ACTIVITIES

More than anything else, the world wide web is a repository of information. Students can research virtually anything under the sun. If something exists in real life, you will certainly find some version of it online.

Below are a few search-based activities which work well in the language classroom.

Try this ☞ **Job applications**

There are literally hundreds of job websites on the world wide web. Some are general (such as monster.com), while others focus on specific job markets such as IT, publishing, law, etc. Review jobs and careers with your class. Ask the students if they have ever attended a job interview. What kind of questions were they asked?

Write the job names on strips of paper and place them in a hat. Split the class into pairs and ask each pair to choose a job. In pairs, the students access an internet job site and search for a job. Ask them to print out and read the job description. Then have them do a role-play – one student plays the interviewer and the other the applicant. You could also video the students' role-plays.

As an alternative activity, have the students write their CVs and apply for a real job of their choice.

Try this ☞ **Electronic field trips**

Not everybody has the time or money to take a trip to some exotic part of the world, but the world wide web can provide the opportunity to take a virtual tour, even if you are not physically there. In fact, the process of exploring a city or museum online appeals to the same physical mode of learning, even if the movement is only virtual.

Try this ☞ **Museums**

Many museums offer interactive websites which allow you to search their collections online and even create your own personal art gallery with items from their collection. Students can simply browse the museum sites randomly and choose their favourite painting for their own galleries. You can also assign specific search tasks, such as finding a painting by a specific artist or looking for an example of a particular art genre.

Here are two activities related to a field trip to an art museum:

Try this ☞ **Art descriptions**

Split your class into small groups. Have each group choose a piece of art from a museum. Together they write a description of the work. Collect the descriptions and put them in a hat. Each group then chooses a description and searches the online collections to find the corresponding piece.

Try this ☞ **Art comparisons**

Ask your students to find works of art that share certain features or subjects, for example, find landscapes of mountains, portraits of women, still-lives with chairs. Students then compare their selected works of art. This can lead to interesting discussions of art genres and history.

Google Earth

One particularly exciting tool to use for visual tours is Google Earth. Google Earth is a programme you can install on your computer which provides satellite pictures of virtually every corner of the world. Type in a location, such as Paris, and you can get satellite views that are close enough for you to see people and cars on a street. You can also get a macro-view of the entire world. Google Earth comes with a variety of fun sub-tools, including tools which allow you to see selected cities in 3D and to see cities through photographs of street scenes as 'real' as if as if you were walking the streets yourself.

Here are a few Google Earth-based activities:

Try this ☞ **Google Earth**

You can use Google Earth as a whole-class whiteboard activity for giving directions. Hand out maps to your students, for instance a map of London. Then open Google Earth and type 'London' into the location search. Invite a student to the front of the class and give them the electronic pen. Choose a location and let the class direct the student to a particular point of interest, for example, Regent's Park. The student can use the pen to zoom into the picture and move along actual city streets until they find the location.

Try this ☞ **A great place to live**

Take your students to Google Earth and let them search for and zoom in on specific areas and/or cities and towns. Your students can talk about their 'dream city' where they would love to live and then find them on Google Earth. Ask them if they can think of any objective criteria for what makes any city a great place to live. Write their ideas on the board. Explain that there are websites which rank cities by their 'liveability'. Give the class the web address of one of these sites (which you can find before class by googling 'cities liveability'). Go over the criteria for 'liveability' listed on the website with the class. Are they the same as the students' ideas? In pairs or small groups, the students can study the rankings of different cities and find what position their dream city occupies. They can prepare and present their findings, using presentation technology such as PowerPoint, wikis, or blogs.

Google Earth activities can easily be combined with activities focusing on travel. Students can use popular travel websites to search for hotels or airline tickets for locations around the world. Try the following fun travel-related activity:

Try this ☞ **Around the world on €5,000**

Tell the students to imagine they each have a budget of €5,000 and a list of cities they have to visit in a period of five days. The students find the cities on Google Earth and explore the resources available, then log onto travel websites and create an itinerary which stays within budget and time. Ask each student (or group of students) to compare their results.

Google also has a further tool, Google Sky, which has mapped the universe as far as we know it. A particularly interesting feature superimposes the constellations on a night sky. This is a good introduction to stories and myths.

For a full list of Google tools, go to www.google.com and search for tools. Google adds new tools on a regular basis, so check the site regularly.

The world wide web

Webquests

Webquests are structured search activities for the world wide web. Unlike treasure hunts, where the core focus is on finding information (for example, finding the distance between two cities, getting departure/arrival times from a timetable, etc.), webquests are centred on a defined task which uses information from the world wide web for a specific purpose. These purposes are directly related to specific higher order thinking skills, such as comparing, analysing, or evaluating – in other words, the search is not an end in itself, but part of the means to solve a problem or support an argument. Webquests are excellent examples of what we call inquiry-based learning.

Well designed webquests encourage technology integration, where the lines between the computer and the classroom lesson blur. If you are in the fortunate position of having multiple computers in your classroom you can quickly send your students to the internet to collect information and then ask them to return to their seats to complete their tasks offline. The web search component of the quest need not take long. If you give clear instructions on where to search, students can find the information they need in a matter of minutes.

One of the greatest challenges for language students using the world wide web lies in one of the web's greatest strengths – its authenticity. Although there are lots of websites aimed at language learners, most webquests involve the use of non-pedagogical websites with ungraded language.

 *Getting it right*

Pre selecting websites for webquests

Consider the following when pre-selecting websites for webquests:

- Accessibility: how quickly can the students access the information? Real content should never be more than three clicks away.
- Language level: is the information at a level your students will understand? Is the information supported with pictures, sound, or other kinds of scaffolding?
- Age appropriacy: scan the website carefully to see if the content is appropriate for your students' ages.

Webquests are task- and content-driven and are not activities generally associated with promoting accuracy. However, it is possible to create very specific criteria for presentation and worksheets which will generate defined chunks of language.

Steps in a webquest

Traditional webquests that are used in mainstream first language education have a very prescribed structure. While you certainly do not need to follow these steps exactly, they do serve as a good reference when designing your web search activity. You can post these steps on a website or give them to the students as a handout. Be sure to discuss each step with the students in detail so that they understand what will happen and what you expect.

Present the context/scenario
Before your students get started, put the task into context. You can do this orally or in written form, as a handout or as part of a website. If, for example, the subject to explore is the weather, brainstorm weather vocabulary and ask students about climates around the world. Spark their interest and get the class focused.

Explain the task
Once the students are interested in the topic, it's time to discuss the overall task and its outcomes. This is very important. Be very clear in your overall goals. A webquest should be more than a series of questions with answers available on the web. Using the weather idea again, the task may be to research weather in two countries and create a presentation comparing conditions in each.

Explain the steps
After the students have been introduced to the goals of the webquest, it's time to go over the specific steps they will need to follow to reach their goal. Most successful webquests are a logical sequence of targeted questions through which students gather information to solve the overall task. Again, you may choose to assign specific websites for the students to explore, or leave this decision to them.

Explain the product and assessment
Define the final outcome of the webquest. Will you require an oral presentation, a PowerPoint presentation, an essay, a wiki, or a blog? How will this final product be evaluated? Since the webquest consists of process and product in equal proportions, you will need to take both into consideration when assigning a grade. A rubric is generally the best way to do this. The rubric criteria will depend on the process and product of your webquest and the overall language aims you seek to achieve through the activity. There are many rubric generators available free on the web, which can make the process of developing a rubric fast and easy (see page 94 of Useful websites for links).

Try this ☞ **Restaurateur**

Tell the students to imagine they are an entrepreneur and want to open a restaurant in the city of Dublin. What kind of restaurant will it be? Where will it be located? They can research locations, buildings, menus, and choose recipes to include on their menu.

Try this ☞ **Choosing a house**

Tell your students to imagine they want to move to a new city. They have to find out the best areas to live and identify houses on the market, choosing one they like within a set budget. They prepare a short presentation on it saying why they like the house and what makes it ideal for them.

Try this ☞ **The world's sport**

In this webquest about football, the students imagine they are the managers of a new world team. They have to investigate past World Cups and put together their greatest team ever. They may have no more than three players from one country. They have to explain who their choices are and why they are good. This activity will also work for other team sports of interest to your students, such as basketball, volleyball, and baseball.

Try this ☞ **The greatest inventions of all**

In this webquest your students have to research great inventions and select five they feel are the most important ever. Alternatively, they can search the web for useless inventions or inventions that have been bad for mankind. Their quest is to find the best or worst inventions and explain why they feel they were important, useless, or bad.

Polls and surveys

Polls and surveys are excellent tools. They generate lots of targeted language practice, encourage critical thinking, and, on a more basic level, provide rich and controversial material for discussions. There are endless examples of polls available on the internet, from very serious, detailed multi-question surveys to simple, funny, one-issue polls. Most poll sites will have a directory of polls you can search through to find one that suits your needs or interests should you decide not to create one of your own. Serious surveys record public opinion on matters ranging from politics to economics to consumer tastes. Silly polls and surveys can include questions such as *Are you ticklish? Would you get a tattoo?*

In short, anything anyone might have an opinion on can be turned into a poll or survey question.

Most language teachers agree that using authentic and personalized materials improves motivation. Using polls and surveys has the added benefit of developing analytical thought and the language used to do the following:

● compare and contrast
● analyse
● summarize
● evaluate.

To familiarize yourself with poll sites, experiment with creating polls on a polling website such as http://www.misterpoll.com/. Create a poll of your choice and create at least five questions using all of the question types available on the site. Send the poll link to a select group of students or colleagues and ask them to complete the poll. Check the results.

Using existing polls and surveys

Students can search for surveys and polls on the internet according to their personal areas of interest. To find a survey on a specific topic, for example, 'football', a search with the words 'survey' and 'football' should give you some useful results. In many cases students can even participate in the polls you find as well as analyse the existing data. As a long-term project, your students can follow polls and surveys over a period of time and note any changes they may observe.

Creating your own poll or survey

Collecting data manually can be a laborious task. You will need to ask yourself if the work involved in setting up an activity is taking time away from other activities in the language classroom. To what extent is the preparatory work even linked to English at all? Internet survey tools simplify the creation process and allow you to use your classroom time to focus on the immediate language task.

There are numerous choices on the web, many of them free. Most allow you to create a variety of question types such as multiple choice, rating scales, or open text fields. You can even add picture prompts to questions. The surveys can be sent via email or made available on a website, for instance as part of a blog or wiki. There are some limitations on free sites, in terms of the number of questions and responses per individual survey, but free surveys are robust enough to serve most classroom needs.

In Screenshot 6.3 is an example of a simple quiz created using one tool, 'Surveymonkey' http://www.surveymonkey.com.

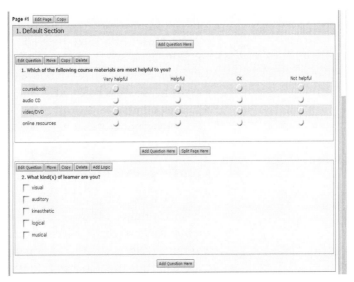

SCREENSHOT 6.3 *Surveymonkey quiz*

Once people have responded to the survey, the website evaluates the responses and provides an automatic report, which you can either display to the class online or print out for students to read (see Screenshot 6.4).

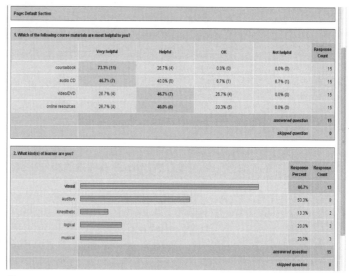

SCREENSHOT 6.4   *Survey report*

Poll and survey ideas

Many poll and survey ideas will come directly from the content of your coursebook. Units on food may well suggest a survey on student likes and dislikes. A unit on greetings and salutations could lead to a cross-cultural survey on customs and traditions. Polls and surveys can be conducted in your class, throughout your school, or across the world. Polls and surveys can form part of a broader cultural exchange or twinning project. They are also really useful as conversation starters.

Polls and surveys can be successfully used in assessment, especially for student self-assessment purposes. At the beginning of the school year you can create a learning styles and student reflection questionnaire. The students can answer questions about how they learn best and what their priorities are for the new school year. This information can be evaluated for the entire class and help you decide how to approach your lessons. You can also use online surveys to allow students to evaluate you and your work and help you in your professional development.

Creating tests and quizzes

Tests and quizzes are related to polls and surveys, however the focus here is measuring right and wrong responses as opposed to opinions. One can argue the value of discreet item testing versus alternative assessment types, but one thing is clear: schools, universities, and other institutions will continue to demand quantifiable results for their students.

The internet offers a wide range of free test creation tools. These tools allow you to create your own tests using a variety of question types, such as multiple choice, drag and drop, and short answer. The test generator software randomizes the questions for you, so you don't have to deliver the same test multiple times. You can choose to print out the test and deliver it in paper and pencil format, or have your students answer the questions online, in which case the computer will generate an automatic score (unless there is an open question, such as a short answer). In Screenshot 6.5 is an example of one test generator in test editing mode:

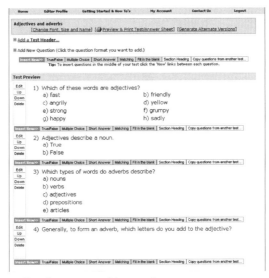

SCREENSHOT 6.5   *Online free test-making tool*

If you don't want to create your own tests, there are a variety of options available either free or at a price. Be sure to check these tests quite closely if you are using them for high-stakes assessment which can have a major impact on a student's future.

Part 4

Using advanced online tools: Web 2.0

7   Web 2.0

Web 2.0 is an umbrella term which refers to a new generation of internet tools. These tools differ from their predecessors in the degree to which they promote connectivity. While in the past, online tools focused on communication (email, texts, chat), content searches (web browsers, search engines) or content creation (websites), the new generation of tools (blogs, wikis, social networks) integrate all these functions and above all link data.

Web 2.0 has democratized content creation, making it possible for virtually anybody to create and quickly share content. Not all Web 2.0 content is new, of course. The digital videos you can view on a website like YouTube have been available on the internet for years. The difference is the accessibility of Web 2.0 sites which allows users to take this content and mix and remix it to create something new.

For language learning, Web 2.0 tools offer great benefits to teachers and students alike, namely:

- They are vast repositories of authentic material in multiple formats (text, photos, pictures, audio, and video).
- They facilitate communication between people around the world with shared interests in a way that email and chat can't.
- They allow students to create their own content quickly and professionally and thereby shift the classroom emphasis from static coursebooks to dynamic tasks.

8 Blogs, wikis, podcasts, and digital portfolios

Of all the new web technologies, blogs and wikis are probably the most common and accepted. They are practical, easy to use, and both require only basic technology skills to create and manage.

A blog is an electronic journal where readers post their thoughts and opinions on a regular basis. It is usually arranged in backwards chronological order, and readers focus on the latest post and read down until they reach the place they left the last time they logged on.

Blogs can be written by individuals, groups, or organizations. Blogs can also be used to host discussions or projects. In a blog, the author shares opinions, insights, and links to related sites of interest that may contain videos, images, audio files (podcasts), or other types of digital media.

The key feature of a blog is the comment function. Only the author of a blog can edit a post, but anyone who has permission to access the blog can comment on what the blogger has written, or comment on the comments of other readers. This makes a blog dynamic and ever-changing, unlike a website, which tends to remain in one constant state for an extended period of time.

In education there are four key types of blog:

1 A teacher blog. This can be used to communicate with students and provide links to resources. For example, the teacher can post homework assignments and links to useful resources. The teacher can also use a blog to manage resources and share with colleagues both local and around the world.

2 Student blogs. These can be used for a variety of writing assignments. They can be managed as the focus of projects by individual students (for example, in the form of an e-portfolio, which we discuss later) or by a small group. True to the original intention of blogs, they can also be a communication tool to share student reflection with the teacher and their peers.

3 Class blogs. These are student blogs for the whole class group. They are particularly useful in twinning projects. A class blog can link to both individual student blogs and teacher blogs.

4 Project or topic blogs. Blogs need not only be defined by their users – the subject of a blog is equally important. You can create a blog for a specific

Blogs, wikis, podcasts, and digital portfolios

topic or a project. The blog can be ongoing, or you can simply delete it when the project is over or you move onto a different topic. Blogs are not designed to be permanent and you can delete and create as many blogs as you like.

To start a blog, go to one of the blog building websites available for free on the internet (for some suggestions, see Useful websites on page 93). Each website has a step-by-step process for you to follow.

In screenshot 8.1 is an example of a blog created by a teacher in New York who uses it to communicate with an entire class and to give assignments.

New York and Other Places
Lists April 9th, 2008

Hello Everbody!

This week we are working on adjectives + adverbs and comparative + superlative structures (comparing one thing to another, or comparing one thing to many things). So let's talk about how our hometowns are different (or similar) to New York City by listing 3 things (or more!) that you find fascinating or strange or really cool about New York City...

I'll go first...

1) New York is much bigger than Montreal and people move at a faster pace.

2) Montreal is much colder and snowier than New York (so stop complaining about the weather here!)

3) New Yorkers are more outspoken and weirder than Montrealers... last week I saw a man walking down the street with an ENORMOUS snake on his shoulders!

... your turn!

Gina

🖵 2 Comments Tagged adjectives, adverbs, comparative, comparing New York, Lists, New York, superlative

SCREENSHOT 8.1   *A teacher's blog*

Below are examples of blogs which have worked in EFL classrooms in different parts of the world. What value can you see in using blogs for these activities?

Try this ☞ **Which job should get paid the most?**

Review the vocabulary of occupations with your students. Ask them what career they would like to pursue when they have finished their education. If your students are advanced, explore the rationale for their decision. Is it the money they can make or the satisfaction the job brings? Ask your students if they feel every job gets paid fairly. As a blog post, have each student identify one job that is overpaid and one that is underpaid and explain why they feel this is so. Each student must make at least three comments on their classmates' blogs.

Try this ☞ **Language learning journal**

Blogs are excellent tools for reflection on learning. Assign a weekly blog post to your students to talk about their learning for the week. What did they learn this week? What was difficult? What did they particularly enjoy? This is a good way to encourage students to write, and as long as you are clear about how often you check the journals, the students will aim to write for an audience.

Try this ☞ **Great sports stars**

Using a student blog, your students can write about their favourite sports stars and provide links to related sites of interest. They can post updates and comments on recent games and invite others to voice their opinions.

↓ WIKIS

A wiki is a tool which allows people to work together on a common webpage. Wikis are built up by a group. They are about collaborative work.

As an introduction to wikis, it is useful to go to the mother of them all – *Wikipedia*. *Wikipedia* is an enormous collection of information, editable by anyone who registers at the site. At the time of writing it is very popular and is available in several languages. The 'group' building it up is international. Teachers and students have to remember though that because anyone can edit content, if you are using it for work where you need to be sure that the facts are accurate, you need to check the information given in *Wikipedia* against other sources.

Try this ☞ **Checking Wikipedia**

Direct the students to the online encyclopaedia, Wikipedia (wikipedia.com). Together, explore how you can register and edit a page. Explain to the students that you want them to look for information about their home country or town and check if what is written is true. If the information they find is true, they can add new details to the entries. If it is not, they can correct it. Make sure you tell the students that they must be factual in their edits and not knowingly post incorrect information or nonsense. Check Wikipedia periodically to see if anyone has edited your students' posts. They can even write a Wikipedia post on a subject they feel they know a lot about.

Returning to small wikis that you can start yourself for use with your students, Screenshots 8.2 and 8.3 show a demo wiki that I created on the wiki service wikispaces.com, to highlight key tools. Other wiki tools may have slightly different terminology, but the basic structures are very similar.

The structure of a wiki is extremely simple. It starts off as a blank page and develops by linking additional pages. The wiki keeps a running record of all changes to all pages.

In the first **screenshot** we are in view mode. In this view we see the current version of the page. If we click on the history tab (two along from 'page' at the top of the screen) we will also see a list of all other versions of the page which we can view. Below the page content there is also a comments box. On the right there is a button to create a new page. This page can then be linked to any other webpage on your wiki or for that matter to any other webpage on the world wide web, as long as the owners of the wiki grant users this permission.

SCREENSHOT 8.2 *Wiki in view mode*

The next screenshot shows edit mode. Here, there is a toolbar much like the one in a conventional word processing programme like Microsoft Word. One very powerful addition to the toolbar is the facility for adding plug-ins to your page. Some plug-ins which are good to start off with are audio or video clips and photos. At the bottom of the screen you save your page with the save button. It then becomes the most recent version you will see in view mode.

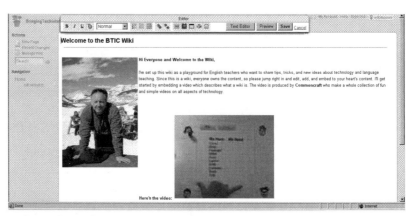

SCREENSHOT 8.3 *Wiki in edit mode*

Wikis and the writing process

A wiki allows all its users to collaborate on a text, saving different versions as the text is developed. For this reason it can be a useful tool to support what is called 'process writing'. Process writing breaks down a writing task into manageable steps which provide structure for student writing tasks. Traditionally, the steps in the writing process have been identified as:

- *Brainstorm* This is when the students all contribute their ideas on a topic, to warm up for the task. This step has no structure. It is for idea-sharing. With wikis, students can create a group brainstorming page for a project. Students can log on and add, edit, or delete ideas without the risk of losing what their peers have created. The teacher can also add comments to the page.
- *Draft* This is the phase where students start organizing their ideas from the brainstorming phase into a coherent text. This may be just an outline or a full first draft. The wiki's facility for saving multiple versions encourages students to take more risks at this stage in their writing, since they know they can easily modify their text later.
- *Revise* The revision phase is for feedback on the piece of writing being created. This feedback comes from a teacher or another student who has been assigned the role of editor. On a wiki, the editor can either use the comment function or add edits into the text itself.
- *Edit* Here the focus is on editing for accuracy – getting spelling correct, making sure appropriate punctuation is being used, etc. The teacher or student editor can edit a page of work and simply highlight errors for correction which the writer then reworks, making the appropriate changes. On a wiki, all the previous versions remain unchanged allowing all participants to go back and review the process step by step.
- *Publish* Finally, when the text is ready to be 'published', there is no need to upload it to a school website or other location, as the wiki itself is the website, so it is already published. Students can make last minute adjustments on the format without fear of making irreversible changes. You can decide what audience you allow to access the students' work – your class alone, parents and teachers, your twinned school, etc.

A class wiki site

As a teacher, you can use a wiki as a class homepage – a place where you can post messages and assignments as well as provide links to resources. You need to create a wiki and then invite all your students (by email) to join. In this way you are using a wiki to pull your students to a central location. As part of your class wiki, each student can create their own profile pages, linked to the wiki homepage. You can choose how specific to be about the content of your students' profile page (see the section below on digital portfolios for more information on this idea).

Wikis can also simply serve as an online place to keep information such as useful links, videos and audio clips, student work, and teacher commentary.

 **Getting it right**

Use RSS feeds to save time on wikis and blogs

Most wiki and blog programmes allow you to generate RSS feeds (see page 50). If you are working with ongoing student blogs, you can save a lot of time by creating RSS feeds from the individual blogs to your reader page. You can then read all the postings in one place, and even post back without having to open and close multiple **windows** in your browser.

Try this ☞ **What's going on?**

Most major cities have online city guides which list entertainment (music, art exhibitions, plays, films). Preselect a set of websites from English-speaking cities (or cities which have English language city guides online). Using a wiki, the students create a series of webpages which can be linked to each other and/or a central homepage as well as outside websites. This is easily done by clicking on the link button on the editing toolbar.

Explain to your students that they are going to plan a fun Saturday evening in an English-speaking city. Elicit categories of activities that can take place in a city (for example, concerts, sports events, restaurant visits), and create an empty wiki page for each category. If possible, do this with the class using an IWB or a computer projector to demonstrate the steps. Split the class into groups so that each group can research what is happening in a particular city on a Saturday night. Assign each group one of the wiki pages you created and ask them to fill it in with the information they collected. As a class, go over each wiki page and encourage groups to add their information to their classmates' wiki pages. This can be done in small groups or as a whole class activity by inviting students to add their content using IWB tools.

Note: this kind of wiki activity can also be done at home or in the computer room outside class time.

Try this ☞ **Student newspaper wiki**

Bring a newspaper to class and review its structure. If possible, present the website of the same newspaper and compare the structure of each. Explain that you want the class to create an online newspaper or newsletter of their own. Decide with the class on sections for your newspaper (sports, news, learning tips, opinion, etc.).

Wikis as collections

Wikis are a very practical tool for collecting information on a particular subject. The fact that any registered user can edit pages means that wikis make great online collaborative projects. Of course, there is the risk that contributors might post incorrect information on the wiki. The teacher can note this and either enter a correction or use the information as a teaching point in class, or the students can be given autonomy in their collaborative work and be instructed to use the wiki's editing function to exercise control over the content. With the history function of the wiki, there is no risk that correct information will be permanently deleted. Prior versions can be reactivated at any time.

Try this ☞ **How to learn a foreign language wiki**

Elicit examples of learning strategies, drawing mind maps to link vocabulary, and invite your students to organize them into logical categories, such as how to learn grammar, or improve reading skills, listening skills, etc. Project an empty wiki onto your IWB and invite students to take turns (individually or in groups) adding to the wiki, creating new pages and content, and linking them together.

Blogs, wikis, podcasts, and digital portfolios

Try this  **Collaborative vocabulary lists**

Create a wiki for your class and display the empty wiki on the IWB (or board, using a projector). Explain to the class that you are going to create an ongoing vocabulary list which every student can contribute to. Decide on the categories you want to organize vocabulary on the wiki. Depending on your classroom situation, your options might be:

- topic area: home, sports, family
- special focus: ESP medical terminology, hospitality
- language area: adjectives, verbs, nouns. These words can in turn be divided up into topic areas.

Create an empty wiki page for each vocabulary category. Split the class into small groups and assign each group a wiki page to work on either in class or at home. Later, reassign the wiki pages so that students from other groups can contribute to other pages.

✓ Getting it right **Choosing between a wiki and a blog**

Many activities could be done on a blog or on a wiki. It depends on where you want to place the emphasis. If you want your students to comment on one central theme, with their comments listed chronologically, choose a blog. If you want the activity to be a project edited by the group, a wiki is better.

In Table 8.1 is a summary of the characteristics of and differences between wikis and blogs:

Blogs	Wikis
• Blogs are based on commentary.	• Wikis are based on editing.
• Once something is posted on a blog only the writer can edit it. Others can only add comments.	• Anyone can edit anything on a wiki page.
• Blogs are organized chronologically.	• Wikis have no predetermined structure (because they are based on hyperlinks).
• Blogs tend to present a particular point of view and are personal.	• Wikis are the product of multiple inputs.
• Blogs are useful for spreading information to the outside and linking with like-minded people or those with shared interests.	• Wikis are useful for developing internal communities and promoting collaboration.

TABLE 8.1 *The differences between blogs and wikis*

↓ PODCASTS

Podcasts provide your students with excellent opportunities to access and create authentic digital audio and video material. But what is a podcast? A podcast is a digital recording delivered in a format that can be played on computer devices such as a desktop computer, a laptop, or a portable media player. The name is derived from the term iPod, the portable media player made by Apple computers, and the word 'broadcast'. Podcasts are different from other types of recordings in that they can be **downloaded** to these mobile players, making them portable for both students and teachers. Using an iPod or other small portable device, you can store literally hundreds of hours of video and audio content which you can use by connecting to any computer capable of playing audio or video files.

Blogs, wikis, podcasts, and digital portfolios

Finding podcasts

Since it is so easy to create podcasts, they are appearing in every area of the world wide web. As with most content on the web, there are good podcasts and bad podcasts, and since everything can look so professional, it is hard to know which is which at first glance. Hence, broad searches can be a bit hit and miss. Conducting some research beforehand can help simplify your search. The first place to look is in one of the larger podcast search sites. In Screenshot 8.4 is a search result using the fairly wide criterion 'EFL' on Apple's iTunes site. The search yielded only 21 results, a manageable number to look through to start.

SCREENSHOT 8.4   *Podcast search results on iTunes*

Once you have found a podcast that is useful for you and your students, you have the option to subscribe to the service. Like RSS feeds, podcast subscriptions automatically update your podcast library each time you log onto your library site, for example iTunes or BBC. This means that every time you log onto your podcast host, you receive a download of the latest version of the podcast.

Creating podcasts

You don't need to be an expert to create your own podcasts. You will find a number of free programmes on the internet. A very popular option in this regard is Audacity (for other audio and podcast websites, see Useful websites, page 93). Audacity is an audio editing programme which allows you to record digital audio and then edit it. It allows you to convert non-digital recordings into digital files. Audacity works much like a traditional recorder with added tools to help you eliminate background noise and add special effects. Once you have created an audio file, you need to save it. Podcasts are saved in the common MP3 format, so you will need to save your audio file in this format. Your audio programme will provide prompts to select the appropriate 'save' format.

Before you start recording, it's important to plan what you want to say. What will the format of the podcast be? Will it be an interview, a commentary, a report, or maybe even a radio play? What about a game show? How many students will be involved? If possible, make a podcasting project collaborative and encourage students to take turns speaking.

Outline the key talking points, but avoid reading from a script. A podcast in an EFL environment should focus on fluency. Encourage your students to take risks. Digital recording can be erased and re-recorded as often as you like.

Once you have a topic and format, you need to be aware of timing. Speaking for two minutes can seem like an eternity for a native speaker, not to mention for a language learner. Limit speaking time for lower-level language learners to 1–3 minutes maximum. Of course, group podcasts with multiple speakers can be longer.

Publishing podcasts

One thing to consider is whether you are really planning to make a podcast or simply a digital recording to play locally from your computer. Podcasts are meant to be broadcast and that means they need to get uploaded to a host website. Many students find it particularly rewarding to have a podcast available on the open web. There are numerous sites on the web that offer hosting to podcasts. Some of these sites also offer the software to create the podcasts themselves.

Podcast ideas

Pretty much anything you can record can be turned into a podcast. The only limitations are your own imagination. Here are some ideas:

Try this ☞ **This week from classroom X**

This project is based on TV and radio talk shows. Each week, students comment on events of the past week. Students can focus on international news, sports, or issues closer to home, such as the topics of their English lessons or what's new in their school. While all students should be encouraged to speak, you will have to limit the number of students actually recording their voices for any given podcast.

Split the class into groups and assign each group responsibility for a particular aspect of the broadcast. Discuss a commentary format with the students. Elicit an organizational structure for a commentary piece and have each small group create a clear outline of what they plan to say. Although only one or two people per group will actually speak on the podcast, the whole group will gain valuable speaking practice preparing for the broadcast.

Blogs, wikis, podcasts, and digital portfolios

Try this ☞ **Creative writing podcast**

Get your students to practise both creative writing and pronunciation by creating spoken podcasts of their creative writing. Students can write and record themselves reading short stories or poems and post them on the web for anyone to read. To focus their efforts, you could choose a particular 'feelings' topic for the students to write and speak about (for example, love and happiness, or loneliness and despair). Alternatively, you could ask your students to create spoken images – descriptions of landscapes, people, or scenes. If you or your students like working with online audio tools you can add background music or record sound effects which you either create by yourself or import from relevant websites (see Useful websites, page 93).

Try this ☞ **The trivia show**

Before class, go to the internet and browse a trivia website and choose a series of questions for the game. Explain that trivia means little known, unusual, and/ or unimportant facts. Give a few examples and see if the students can guess the answers. Divide the class into teams and each team into a show presenter and three or four contestants. The presenter leads the show and asks the questions. Use a bell or a kitchen timer to signal the beginning and end of contestant turns. Ensure that each team has a chance to play the game.
Note: you can also record the show but be sure to manage the noise level and interruptions.

↓ DIGITAL PORTFOLIOS

Portfolios are examples of student work, documenting student learning over time. Portfolio assessment is one of the most popular forms of alternative assessment in the language classroom, at least in principle. In real life, portfolio assessment has followed a much more difficult road to acceptance. Teachers and students often complain about the physical size of portfolios and the awkwardness of handling and storing them. As a result, portfolios have been implemented haphazardly, with varying degrees of depth, intensity, and success.

Electronic portfolios offer a far less complicated and more easily managed alternative. Rather than storing reams of paper, student portfolios become electronic files hosted on websites or stored locally on computer hard drives.

The European Language Portfolio

The *European Language Portfolio (ELP)* is perhaps the most widely accepted and well known portfolio assessment tool in the language teaching world. With its introduction, keeping a language learning portfolio has been 'officially sanctioned' and has become, again, at least in principle, an official document, with the validity of a test or exam.

This portfolio, which is approved by the Council of Europe, is broken down into three key sections:

• A Language Passport (listing official transcripts, exams)

- A Language Biography (which includes learning goals, can-do statements, and self-assessment)
- A Dossier (which contains a body of work reflecting student learning and achievement).

There have been numerous projects to develop digital versions of this portfolio. Most of these versions are available for free (see Useful websites, page 00).

Creating your own portfolio

Many teachers prefer to create their own portfolios rather than use a template such as the *European Language Portfolio*. If you choose this route, consider the following steps:

1   Define the purpose of the portfolio. There are two basic types of portfolios:

- Working portfolios, demonstrating work in progress and focusing on reflection
- Presentation portfolios, showing examples of complete work and aimed at demonstrating ability or competence in a particular area.

Think about who will read the portfolios. Perhaps the students will show them to their parents. Will the portfolio be part of a final grade?

2   Organize the portfolio. How do you want to segment the portfolio? Will you divide the work up by topic area? Perhaps you want the work to be related to a particular skill or, to use the more modern term, a can-do statement?

3   Choose the appropriate technology. Digital portfolios can be created with any number of technology tools, from a word processing programme, to PowerPoint, to wikis and blogs. Your decision will necessarily be influenced by your local situation (if internet access is difficult, do not choose wikis or blogs) and the personal preferences and skills you and your students bring to the classroom.

4   Create a folder with all examples of work. Rather than adding a piece of student's work to each individual page of a portfolio, it makes more sense to create an archive of all work. You can then link from a portfolio page to your work, or, if you wish to display (or embed) the work, you can simply upload selected files from the archive location.

 *Getting it right*

Back up project work

Backing up your work (saving it to a portable disk) requires little effort but can make a big difference when you are working on a long-term project such as a portfolio. If you don't have a back-up hard disk you can use a CD or a thumb-drive as insurance in case anything happens to your computer. There are also numerous online back-up sites where you can save the files on your computer.

Blogs, wikis, podcasts, and digital portfolios

Digital portfolio using a wiki

A wiki is a very useful tool for creating a digital portfolio. Because of its editing function, it is easier to manipulate and change than, for example, a blog. The 'history' function automatically allows viewers to trace progress over time rather than simply displaying only the final product. Thus, in a wiki format, you can have a working portfolio showing drafts and a presentation portfolio with a final product, all in the same document. The flexibility of hyperlinking allows students to be creative in designing their portfolio site. Students can create a series of introductory pages to form a core navigational structure for their portfolio and add content directly onto a page or link it to examples of work stored elsewhere. Using a wiki portfolio, your students can each work on their own version of a portfolio document that you have loaded. The interactivity of the wiki also makes a portfolio a far more dynamic document, with both teacher and student having access to each page.

9   Social networks

↓ WHAT ARE SOCIAL NETWORKS?

The core idea behind social networks is to create a common space where people with shared interests can exchange ideas, experiences, and information. Some social networks have been created based on content areas such as lovers of football, cooking enthusiasts, students of English, or people from a particular city, but the large communities, such as MySpace, Facebook, or YouTube, have created a space for self-expression which is not bound by specific topics or interests. Within the larger community, smaller 'interest groups' emerge as members make 'friends' who in turn have 'friends', each one with their own set of interests and sub-conversations going on.

↓ SECURITY ON THE INTERNET ON WEB 2.0 APPLICATIONS

Earlier we talked about internet security and steps you can take to protect yourself, your computer, and your data. When dealing with social networks and Web 2.0 we need to look at security again.

Social networks can be used to positive effect in countless ways in teaching and learning. However, there are risks inherent in sharing and collaborating online, which go beyond viruses, worms, and identity theft. When you and your students use a social website, a part of your identity necessarily goes online. As you link to 'friends' who in turn have friends, and friends of friends, your information can travel around the world.

If you educate yourself and your students on internet safety, you can limit that risk and have an enriching experience using Web 2.0 tools. Below are some key points to consider:

- Have your students sign an internet code of conduct. Many internet safety groups such as BECTA (www.becta.org.uk) in the UK have sample documents you can use as examples. Awareness is the first step towards internet security. Another internet safety group is www.isafe.org, a non-profit group in the USA.
- Explore the structure of the social networking site you are considering using. Can you adjust privacy settings? Nowadays, most major social networking sites have privacy settings which can limit the people who have access to your information. Be sure to check that your students have set their profiles to private. Luckily, many social websites are now setting profile defaults to private.

Social networks

- Even if you control access to your network, only post information you are comfortable showing to other people. Remember that once something is posted publicly online you can't get it back. Even if you delete the information it can still be sitting locally on someone's computer. Make sure your students understand this.
- Don't share passwords and when creating passwords take care to make them 'strong'. Strong passwords are complex and make it hard for hackers to break. Here are some tips for creating strong passwords:
  - Make your password long.
  - Mix numbers, letters, and special characters.
  - Substitute symbols or numbers for letters (ye$ for yes, !ndia for India).
  - Use a word or phrase that only you can understand.

You can check the strength of your password by going to http://www.microsoft.com/protect/yourself/password/checker.mspx

- Create usernames that do not give hints to your real identity.
- Consider using a new email account (hotmail, googlemail, and yahoomail all offer free accounts) to set up your online account. That way, if your information is compromised your central email account is still protected.
- If you are working on social networking sites in a language lab, be sure that you and your students always log out after a session.
- Using large open social networks also presents the risk of students accessing inappropriate content. Most social websites do not allow students under 13 to create profiles and this should be a minimum age limit for children to surf these sites as well.

↓ USING SOCIAL NETWORKS IN EFL TEACHING

Social networks provide rich opportunities to use English in a targeted, purposeful way. In fact, each step in the process of using the network creates multiple opportunities for authentic communication. Below are two steps common to most social networking sites.

1 *Create a profile*. All social network services will ask the user to create a profile, asking for some personal information.

2 *Find friends*. Once you have created a profile, the next logical step is for the students to look for 'friends' who share similar interests. You can either search through a list of groups for friends already on the network or you can invite a non-member through email. Once the user finds a group that meets their interests, they can join and participate in discussions or engage with individual members and invite them to be their friends. They can also create their own new groups.

Note: you will not be able to correspond directly with a prospective friend until that friend agrees and approves the request.

You can use the IWB to show your students how you are creating your profile, then ask them to create theirs and to join your network.

Social networks

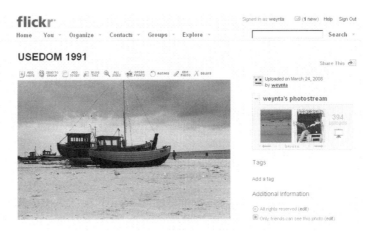

SCREENSHOT 9.1   *Flickr website*

Some social networks are image-based, and allow you to post and share photographs, videos, and animation free. One such website at the time of writing is www.flickr.com (see Screenshot 9.1), which is an easily searchable database of images where each picture is tagged with certain searchable **keywords**. (For more image-sharing networks, see Useful websites, page 94).

The advantage of image-sharing networks is that they enable you to create folders of images for your students to work with at their own computer or for the class to use together on the IWB. Using an image-sharing network will save you hours of time searching for appropriate images and also save you money on copying and other reproduction costs. These image-sharing networks function in much the same way other social networks do. You create a profile, find friends, or join groups.

Organizing pictures on flickr is quick and straightforward. Before you start, organize the files on your computer into easy-to-find folders. After you log onto flickr and go to the 'upload images' button on the home page, select 'choose photos' and locate and click on the photos you choose to upload. Remember, holding down the left button of your mouse will allow you to select multiple images. At this point a list of your selected photos will appear on the flickr site. You can set your privacy level so that only you and your friends can access it, and click 'upload'. You then have a further option at this point to state whether you want your gallery to be accessible to online searches or not. You can now add tags and descriptions of your photos and add them to sets (galleries) or create a new gallery for these photos.

If you are in a hurry, you can always edit pictures and move them around later. Simply click on 'organize' and choose what you want to work on.

Here are some activities that work quite well with flickr:

Try this ☞ **Guess where/ Guess what**

Use images to practise the language of opinion and speculation (*I think it's .../ It must be .../ It can't be ...*). Select images (or upload your own photos onto the site for the class) and have students guess where the image was taken or what

Social networks

the image actually shows. This is a particularly fun activity for students to do as group or pairwork.

Try this ☞ **Photo exchange with another class/school**

You can use the closed group function of flickr to share safely photos and commentary with another class in your school or a twinned school with which you already have links.

Try this ☞ **Create a photo story**

Upload your images to your flickr address. Click on the 'set' button and select images to form a story. Under each picture students create text for the story. Classmates can peer correct or make suggestions by using the commentary function that comes with each picture.

↓ VOICETHREAD

Voicethread is a free online tool which allows students to create presentations which combine images with commentary in the form of text or audio. It is really easy to use and since it is based online, it does not require any downloads to work. Voicethread is very flexible. It allows users to upload images, videos, and text from a local computer or common social sites such as flickr or YouTube. These images then become pages in a Voicethread presentation. The creator of the media album can then write comments which are attached to each page. In turn, viewers can add additional comments to the presentation, making it an interactive experience. The creator of the media album can delete comments, as they retain control of the media album.

One great innovation of Voicethread is the possibility it provides to post comments via webcam, live audio recording, audio files, or typed-in text. This is a particularly useful tool to help students practise their speaking skills. The commentary function allows learners to engage in a digital conversation anchored by the image presentation. Since the discussion is asynchronous, students have time to reflect and develop their responses – an important factor for language learners.

Presentations

Assign students a topic for a presentation, for example, 'My home town'. Students upload relevant images and record their commentary. They can make their own multi-page descriptions, or be responsible for an individual page in a class presentation. At the time of publication, a good example of an EFL class presentation by a class in Brazil is available on Voicethread: http://voicethread.com/#q.b69307.i359512. Below are some ideas on using Voicethread.

Try this ☞ **Storytelling**

Students can choose a series of images and create a story, with a spoken narrative, using the 'commentary' function. Alternatively, you yourself can select an image and ask the students to use the commentary function to comment. In this case the presentation can contain a single page with multiple comments.

Try this ☞ **Student portfolios**

Students can submit texts, videos, and/or audio commentaries to Voicethread, making their personal portfolio of information on a given topic. Teachers then evaluate and post comments directly to the presentation.

Try this ☞ **Instructions**

Before class, take and upload three sets of photos showing simple processes: these could be on a cookery theme, for example making a cake, or a functional theme, for example giving directions, or a technology theme, for example. making a wiki, or any other theme you like. Using the story function, create a simple Voicethread file and note the URL. In class, divide the class into three groups and give one URL to each group for them to access the photos. Each group's task is to give instructions for each step via the commentary function, to show to the rest of the class.

↓ CREATE YOUR OWN SOCIAL NETWORK

Your students are likely to be familiar with the giant leading social networks like Facebook and Bebo. You can use their interest in social networks, as well as the advantages of social networks themselves by creating your own social network for use as a class. A private, closed social network that you create ensures that only your students join. At the time of writing, the company Ning is a popular platform that offers this service. After entering initial information about your network you can simply drag and drop the features you want onto your site.

Creating a social network on Ning is very straightforward and can be very practical to use with your students (see Screenshots 9.2 and 9.3). The programme guides you through the process in a step-by-step fashion. During this process you can create simple features and define the appearance of your network. Once you have done this, take some time to explore the options you can find under the 'manage' tab on your network main page. This is the control panel that you will use to control and customize the settings of your network. Experiment with the options. You can easily reverse any action you take.

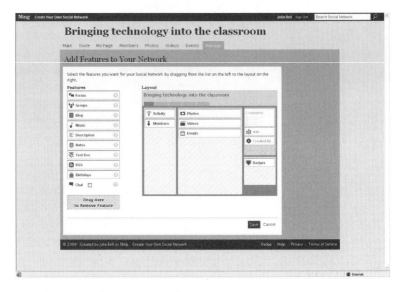

SCREENSHOT 9.2   *Creating a social network on Ning*

Once you have decided on the features you want to have displayed, you can begin adding content to the site. Then, when you are ready to 'open for business' you can invite your class to join the network.

SCREENSHOT 9.3   *A Ning social network homepage*

One very useful feature of a ning is that each member can create a richly featured personal page including a blog (see Screenshot 9.4).

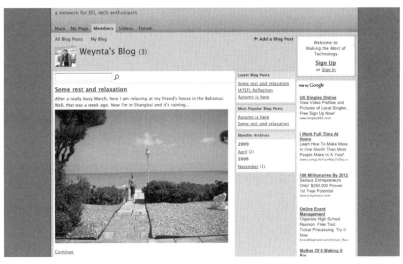

SCREENSHOT 9.4   *The author's blog within a Ning social network*

This is a good alternative for students who do not like the collaboration inherent in using a wiki. Currently Ning does not have an integrated wiki feature, but it is easy enough to link out to a wiki site of your choice to conduct a wiki activity. However, the focus of the ning is less about collaborative content creation than about sharing content and communicating on a common platform.

One of the great things about social networks is their ability to link information from multiple sources on a single profile page. When you create your profile you may want to include a video clip you have found that will be useful for your students, or share some photographs from a collection you have stored on flickr. Of course, you can share links through a site like de.licio.us.com and let people know what you are doing through a twitter feed. If your class is conducting a poll on a polling site, you can add a link to your poll on your network's home page for all members to complete. This is a useful way to elicit discussion.

Think of your social network profile as a compilation rather than a single fixed page.

10   Virtual learning environments

Virtual Learning Environments (VLEs) are software programmes designed to manage, track, and administer learning. Using VLEs, teachers and administrators can create courses, register students, assign tasks, and monitor progress.

VLEs are large and fairly complex programmes. They are solutions for institutions and organizations, not for individual classes. There are many VLEs to choose from, some of which require a fee, such as the popular Blackboardwww.blackboard.com, and others which are free (**open source**) such as Moodle (www.moodle.org). Moodle is particularly popular in education. Once it is set up, it is easy to use for both teachers and students. But unlike Blackboard and other fee-based options, Moodle currently offers no direct technical support, so you will need to have a technology expert on site or hire a Moodle specialist to set things up and to troubleshoot.

VLEs can be used to host online courses, or combined options which mix classroom instruction and online coursework. This is a particularly appealing solution for language learning. Taking advantage of a VLE for practice and even presentation can free up limited class time for real communicative tasks.

A VLE should not be confused with actual course content. The VLE is the infrastructure to which course activities and resources are added. Teachers can attach Word documents, presentations, audio and video files, and of course, links to external websites to their online lessons. In addition, most VLEs also provide tools for online text and video chats as well as for creating wikis and blogs and a variety of question types for tests and quizzes.

With the growth of social computing, VLEs have been criticized for not being learner centred. Opponents say that VLEs are tools to control learning rather than instruments aimed at empowering students to manage their own education. While there is some truth in this, it is indisputable that VLEs can simplify the lives of teachers and students and provide access to learning at any time of day or night. Ultimately, it is the tasks that teachers set which will determine the learner centredness of the programme, not the platform on which it is built.

Should you use a VLE? After all, you can post all kinds of documents to a wiki or publish answers to assignments on a blog. You can also create tests and quizzes free and then link them to a website, wiki, or blog. What you can't do is measure class progress easily. What a VLE can do for you is store your class data in areas of the VLE which are staff-accessible only and generate reports quickly and efficiently. If you work in an institution with rigorous assessment requirements, the VLE can speed up administrative tasks and provide real-time data that can help you to identify student trends and potential problems.

As we said earlier, VLEs are not individual solutions. Opting for a VLE needs to take place at an institutional level. Implementing the VLE will take a lot of planning and coordination and will not take place overnight.

Virtual learning environments

Part 5 Looking forward

11 Technology and differentiation

No two learners are completely alike. Each student brings a unique mix of learning styles to the language classroom. It is a huge challenge for teachers to identify these learning styles and design activities which appeal to the class as a whole and yet take into account the individual needs of each student.

Technology is a powerful tool that you can use to differentiate your classroom instruction and address individual learner needs. There is a strong correlation between student learning styles and technology options.

For learners who are logical thinkers, tools such as online polls and surveys would be appealing.

Those who are visual learners would enjoy working with digital cameras, video, and online resources such as Google Earth.

Learners with a strong reflective side will feel comfortable blogging or building an e-portfolio.

Social learners will enjoy chatting, email, and social network sites.

Even very physical (kinaesthetic) learners have technology-based options such as 3D worlds, virtual tours, and animation.

This relationship between learning styles and technology tools can be applied to a specific activity such as working with a story. You and your students have many options:

- read the story from a screen or print it out
- read the story and listen to an audio recording at the same time
- read a story with accompanying pictures
- read a story with pictures and audio
- watch an animation of the story
- watch a video of the story

Your class can also create all of the above for an existing story or for a story they compose on their own.

Of course, technology will only have a positive impact on differentiation if the tools available are used selectively. If you send your entire class to a language lab to do the same activity on rows of computers, you will not be appealing to different learning styles. Vary the tasks you assign your students or, within these tasks, vary the roles each student performs. Using technology to diversify instruction requires imagination and diversity in its application.

12   The future

Whenever you publish a book about technology you run the risk of being a bit behind the times by the time the book goes to print. Predicting the future of technology is very difficult. Powerful new applications are emerging on a daily basis.

However, there are certain trends that will certainly inform the use of educational technology in the immediate future. One area that holds a lot of promise is the concept of Personal Learning Environments (PLEs) (see Screenshot 12.1). Taking a step beyond traditional VLEs, in the personal learning environments of the future, students will have an array of tools at their disposal which will allow them to be masters of their own learning process. The classroom and the course materials attached to it will be just a part of a much broader learning space which will include portfolios, relevant links, discussion groups, and outlets for opinions and comments like blogs.

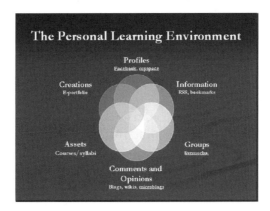

SCREENSHOT 12.1   *The Personal Learning Environment*

In the future, students will receive course materials that match their personal interests as defined in their self-generated profiles. Online tests and quizzes will generate individually structured study exercises for student practice.

For teachers and administrators, the new tools will give schools flexibility of delivery. Schools will be able to choose to teach certain elements online and others in the face-to-face classroom. With course materials delivered in modular online units, schools will be able choose to print out some units and leave others online.

Another development with far-reaching impact for the future is 'cloud computing'. The 'cloud' is a popular metaphor for the internet. When you go online and access the internet through a web browser, the information is not on your computer in the way your documents and applications are, but somewhere undefined – in the clouds. In cloud computing, even your desktop will move to the ether. There will be no need to license software and download it onto your computer, because the application will be online. Google apps http://www.google.com/apps/ is the most popular example of this kind of internet-based productivity service, where you can create documents, presentations, and websites, communicate via email, chat, and manage a calendar – in short do everything a normal suite of office applications can do.

↓ WHAT DOES THIS MEAN FOR YOU?

In the future there will be less need to invest in hardware and software.

Classroom computers will become simplified internet terminals. Not only will you create documents online – you will save them there too. Cloud utilities will provide safe storage for your data. Safe on the internet? Yes, really. Your data will be stored online, divided up into pieces and stored in multiple locations. This makes your data much harder to steal since there is no obvious target.

In the future there will be a greater need to invest in internet bandwidth. You can think of your connection to the internet as a pipe. If all your data and work is going to take place online, you will need a pipe large enough to handle a high flow of information without clogging up. This is probably something your workplace will deal with but it's worth knowing.

Mobile technology will play an ever-increasing role in how students learn. Today's students are always connected and this needs to be acknowledged in education. Learning can take place anytime, anywhere. Students can listen to podcasts or watch videos while taking the bus to school. They can do quizzes or practise vocabulary via their mobile phone and, of course, they can text and chat. While all of these applications are available today, in the future we will integrate mobile technology directly into the instructional model, bringing the world into the classroom in real time. Our mobile phones will be learning hubs enabling us to learn from anywhere, anytime. Just consider the teaching opportunities mobile video and audio recording afford. With the ongoing convergence of social and mobile technology, uploading instantly from a mobile device to a central server will be a matter of a few simple clicks.

In the classroom, mobile technology is already having an impact. Interactive handheld devices allow students to vote and text each other. Portable tablet-like interactive pads link to IWB software and bring the whiteboard to students rather than making students go to the whiteboard – a great option for group work.

A recent study by the Pew Charitable Trust estimates that by the year 2020, 50 per cent of internet users will never have used a computer to access the world wide web. Instead, their mobile phones will be their access point.

The future

Considering that there are approximately 900 million computers in use today, but a staggering 2.7 billion mobile phones scattered across the globe, improving connectivity through mobile devices seems only logical. With prices lower than those of computers, mobile technology will certainly help to bridge the digital divide.

Manage technology, don't let technology manage you. Remember that mobile phones, IWBs, wikis, blogs, podcasts, and word processing applications are all tools to help you and your students be more productive. They are not ends in themselves. Even the content on authentic websites will not constitute learning moments until you create the learning tasks which make your student work with this information in a purposeful way.

It is important to understand the basics of technology to give you the confidence to make informed choices for your classes – to choose the most appropriate tools for your students and the language learning goals you set. Hopefully, this book will be a useful introduction that will help you in this process.

Glossary

Aggregator An application that collects content from multiple websites in one place. Interesting websites can be added to the aggregator, which is also called a **reader**.

Application A computer programme that performs a specific function. Word processing programmes, web browsers, and media players are all applications.

Bandwidth The amount of information that can be sent over a network at any given time. Bandwidth is similar to a motorway: the less traffic there is, the more smoothly and rapidly it flows. Heavy traffic causes traffic jams and delays. Digital data, particularly video data, require considerable bandwidth to run smoothly.

Bookmark (or favourite) A shortcut that saves addresses of websites. Bookmarks are saved by a computer's web browser and eliminate the need to type in long and complicated web addresses.

Boolean operators Used in web searches to refine search results. They key Boolean operators are: AND, NOT, OR. Boolean operators are at the heart of computer programming logic and drive computer reasoning.

Broadband Refers to high-speed data transmission. There are many broadband systems such as DSL or ISDN. These systems are delivered via telephone and cable television lines and provide increased bandwidth, allowing smooth use of multimedia such as video.

Browser A programme that reads website content such as text, images, links, etc. and displays it on a computer. It does this by reading HTML code. Popular web browsers include Microsoft Internet Explorer, Mozilla Firefox, Safari (for Apple computers), and Google Chrome.

Cloud utilities Web-based applications which manage your resources, much like Windows does on a desktop computer.

Downloading The process by which a file is moved from a location on a network to a particular computer to. The opposite action is **uploading**.

Emoticons Icons frequently used in emails and text chats to express a writer's feelings. Emoticons can be individual icons like a smiley face or a combination of keys to produce a picture, e.g. ☺ is made of the : and) signs.

Firewall Protects a computer from malicious intent by filtering data and only allowing safe content to pass. Basic firewalls often come pre-installed on computers but can be added to by security software which monitors incoming activity and blocks content according to customized definitions, by blocking specific websites from accessing information. Most organizations with networks have firewalls installed at the network level.

Flash The name of an animation technology developed by the company Macromedia. It permits programmers to create complex animations which take up little disk space, allowing them to download quickly on common computers. In order to see Flash animation, you need to have a Flash player. Most browsers have a built-in Flash player, but if not, it can be downloaded free from www.macromedia.com.

Hard drive A hard drive is a set of platters on which information is stored magnetically. It is normally the largest storage space on a computer and the place where most applications and system software are stored. The hard drive is the mechanism used to read and write data to and from the hard disk.

Hyperlinks Connections that take the user from one place to another in a document, website, or across the world wide web. A hyperlink can be set under a word, passage, or image. When the link is clicked, the user will be taken to the corresponding page or location. Links can often be recognized in text because they are usually blue and underlined. They also occur in many common documents, especially in tables of contents and glossaries, and enable much quicker browsing than scrolling or text input would allow.

Intranet A private closed network of computers. Many companies and schools have their own intranets, with information and resources for their members. Intranets are protected by network firewalls.

Java A programming language developed by Sun Microsystems. It can be used across computer platforms, making it very practical for use on websites. Small programmes embedded on websites, known as applets, are created using Java.

Keywords Describe content and can be used in search engines to find content, or can be 'tagged' to the content of a website, a section, or an individual object. Keywords, or meta-tags, are a core organizational principle in databases and most social networking sites.

Megapixel Pixel is short for 'picture element' and describes the dots that make up a picture on a computer or digital TV screen. A megapixel is one million pixels. The more megapixels available, the higher the resolution and the clearer the picture on the computer screen.

Modem A device that allows computers to communicate via telephone lines. Most modern computers have built-in modems, but external modems are also available. Older, dial-up modems are increasingly being replaced by ISDN, DSL, or cable options that are much faster and make downloading video and other multimedia easier and more efficient.

MP3 Compressed audio files. The music files downloaded onto a computer, telephone, or portable device are MP3s. They are much smaller than other audio files, yet provide the same sound quality.

Network The connection between two or more computers. Networks come in many formats from household wireless local area networks (LANs), to company-wide **intranets**, to the largest of networks, the internet itself.

Open source Software that allows its code (programming) to be freely distributed and modified. The open source movement is very popular on the internet and there are open-source alternatives to most commercial software programmes. Open-source developers tend to group themselves into communities to share updates and modifications with each other.

Operating system (system software) The operating system of a computer that performs all the essential functions necessary for it to operate such as running applications, managing memory, selecting disk drives, etc. Windows, Macintosh, and Linux are common operating systems.

PDF PDF stands for Portable Document Format. The PDF format allows users to view a document regardless of the software installed on their computer. In order to view PDFs, an *Adobe PDF reader* needs to be installed, which can be downloaded free from www.adobe.com.

Plug and play Devices that operate automatically on a computer, without any need to download specific software or drivers or configure the computer. Plug and play devices commonly are connected through the computer's USB port. Most keyboards, mice, and USB sticks are examples of plug and play devices.

Plug-ins Small add-ons to a computer that allow for increased functionality. A Flash player or Windows media player enhance the functionality of the computer's browser. Other plug-ins can enhance specific applications on the computer. With every browser update, new plug-ins are being integrated into the browser's standard set of features.

QuickTime A multimedia technology developed by Apple Computers. In order to view QuickTime audio and video, it is necessary to install a QuickTime player on the computer, which can be downloaded free from www.apple.com

Reader A application which collects the content from multiple websites in one place. Interesting websites can be added to the reader, which is also called an **aggregator**.

Screenshot A 'photograph' of whatever is on a computer screen at a given moment. Screenshots are images and can be pasted into documents to support a text or provide an example.

Scroll bar A bar down the right-hand side and/or the bottom of a window which enables more of a webpage or document to be seen. A mouse is used to click or drag on the scrollbar to move through and reveal material that is not displayed in the initial window.

Search engines Google, Excite, Lycos, AltaVista, Infoseek, and Yahoo! are all search engines. They index millions of sites on the world wide web, so that surfers can find the sites and information they want more easily by using search terms or phrases.

Toolbar A set of buttons used to access the functions of a computer desktop, an application, or a website. Many applications, such as word processing programmes, have multiple toolbars depending on the type of action needing to be performed.

Uploading The process by which a file is moved from a computer to another location on a network. It is the opposite of downloading.

URL Stands for Uniform Resource Locator and is the equivalent of an address for a page on the web.

Viruses Malicious programmes and scripts which can have a disastrous impact on a computer. Viruses can do anything from slowing down a system, to mixing up or potentially destroying files. Like human viruses, computer viruses can multiply quickly and spread across a network, infecting all unprotected computers. Viruses are often spread and released by email attachments. Since new viruses are introduced every day, it is important to subscribe to a security service which updates protection regularly in response to new threats.

Webcam Small video cameras with software that allows a user to broadcast video on the web. Webcams are often used in chats and video-conferencing situations.

Website A group of hyperlinked webpages that come together to form an entity on the world wide web. A website can contain anything from a single page to thousands of interconnected pages. The larger the website the more space it takes up on a server.

Wireless internet (or Wi-Fi) A term used for wireless computer networks that allow computers to connect with each other without cables, via radio waves.

Window A rectangular area on a computer screen, which displays content from an application. Multiple windows may be opened on a computer screen, displaying content from a webpage, a word processing document, or a spreadsheet. It is possible to hide, move, stack, and resize windows, and also to navigate between windows by clicking on them. The last window clicked on comes to the front of the stack and is the active window.

World wide web (www) The world wide web is the part of the internet that can be accessed via a web browser. Although often used as if synonymous with the internet, it is actually only one part of it.

Zip (or compressed) Files that are grouped together to create an archive. These take up much less space than individual files and make sending multiple documents via email much faster.

Useful websites

Audio and podcasts
http://audacity.sourceforge.net/
www.powergramo.com/
(Powergramo allows you to record skype conversations)
www.skype.com
http://podcast.com/
www.podcastalley.com
www.betteratenglish.com
www.englishcaster.com
www.wavosaur.com
www.free-sound-editor.com/

Blog building sites
http://edublogs.org/
https://www.blogger.com/start
http://wordpress.com/
www.xanga.com/

Digital language portfolios
www.coe.int/portfolio
www.eelp.org/eportfolio/
www.dilaport.utu.fi/students.htm
http://lolipop-portfolio.eu/
http://electronicportfolios.org/

ELT blogs
www.eflblogs.com/
http://larryferlazzo.edublogs.org/
http://nikpeachey.blogspot.com/
www.writeit.fi/ruth/
www.freetech4teachers.com/
http://blog-efl.blogspot.com/
www.ihes.com/bcn/tt/eltblog/blog/

ELT resources
www.bbc.co.uk/worldservice/learningenglish/
www.britishcouncil.org/central.htm
www.malhatlantica.pt/teresadeca/school/efl-eslpage.htm
http://languagelearningcentre.wordpress.com/2007/09/03/
www.eslbase.com/resources
www.onestopenglish.com
www.linguistlist.org/sp/LangLearnESL.html
http://iteslj.org/

Freeware
www.adobe.com/
www.apple.com/
www.winzip.com/

General technology resources
www.internet4classrooms.com/esl.htm
www.technorati.com/
http://coolcatteacher.blogspot.com/
www.webheadsinaction.org/
www.call4all.us/
www.teach-nology.com/

Image-sharing networks
www.flickr.com/
www.zooomr.com/
www.photobucket.com/

Interactive whiteboard
http://smarttech.com/
www.prometheanworld.com/
(see subsite, Promethean Planet, for IWB ideas)
www.mimio.com/
http://tinyurl.com/s988m
www.schoolzone.co.uk/resources/IWB/

Online lessons
http://daily-english-activities.blogspot.com/
www.avatarlanguages.com/
www.breakingnewsenglish.com/
www.splendid-speaking.com/

Polls and surveys
www.ciser.cornell.edu/info/polls.shtml#multi
www.zoomerang.com/
www.surveymonkey.com/

Projects
www.globalschoolnet.org/GSH/pr/
www.iearn.org/

Public domain content
http://search.creativecommons.org/
http://wikisource.org/
www.gutenberg.org/

Rubrics
www.etni.org.il/standards/abtrubrics.htm
http://rubistar.4teachers.org/
www.rubrician.com/
http://edorigami.wikispaces.com/

Security on the internet

www.ceop.gov.uk
www.thinkuknow.co.uk
www.getnetwise.org

Social bookmarking

http://digg.com/
http://delicious.com/
http://buzz.yahoo.com/

Social networks

www.flickr.com/
www.ning.com
www.odeo.com
http://secondlife.com/
http://twitter.com/
www.youtube.com

Tutorials

www.commoncraft.com/
http://nikpeachey.blogspot.com/2008/06/create-your-own-social-network-7-steps.html
www.internet4classrooms.com/on-line.htm
http://office.microsoft.com/training

Video

http://video.google.com/
www.youtube.com
www.imdb.com/Sections/Trailers/
www.teflclips.com/
www.videojug.com/

Webquests

http://webquest.org/
www.zunal.com/

Widgets

www.google.com/ig/directory?synd=open
www.widgetbox.com

Wikis

www.wikimatrix.org/
http://pbwiki.com/
www.wetpaint.com/
www.wikispaces.com/
http://educationalwikis.wikispaces.com
http://wiki.classroom20.com/